DUE REVERENCE

Antiques in the Possession of the
American Philosophical Society

DUE REVERENCE

Antiques in the Possession of the American Philosophical Society

Murphy D. Smith
David Borodin, Consultant,
of Frisk and Borodin Appraisers, Ltd.

The American Philosophical Society
Philadelphia, Pennsylvania

Memoirs of the
AMERICAN PHILOSOPHICAL SOCIETY
Held at Philadelphia
For Promoting Useful Knowledge
Volume 203

Library of Congress Catalog Card Number 87-72862
International Standard Book Number 0-87169-203-1
US ISSN 0065-9738

We have no right to despise the discoveries or improvements which have originated in the minds of our contemporaries; yet it is an unscrupulous intellect that does not pay to antiquity its due reverence. . . . There are many kinds of genius; each age has its different gifts.

Preface to *Works of Hilary* by Desiderius Erasmus   (1523)

TABLE OF CONTENTS

PREFACE

This volume evolved from a tiny segment of my study of the Cabinet of Curiosities of the American Philosophical Society. One of the divisions of this Cabinet is "*Objets d'Art*" and I included furniture in this division. As time passed, awareness grew of several fascinating and valuable antiques in the Society, beginning with 1769. Most of the *objets* pertain to various presidents of the Society, although a few are from members whose activity in the Society was memorable. Some items were purchased, also, or made, for the Society.

No work has been done hitherto on this furniture as a unit. Several pieces are well known and have been researched at various times: Franklin's library chair, the Rittenhouse astronomical timepiece, the chair which Jefferson purchased in Philadelphia in 1776 and used while he wrote the Declaration of Independence, for example. Little is known of most of the various artifacts, however, or their provenance.

Considerable reliance has been placed on *A Catalogue of Instruments and Models in the Possession of the American Philosophical Society*, by Robert Multhauf, for descriptions of the mechanisms of the various timepieces. Also, *A Catalogue of Portraits and Other Works of Art in the Possession of the American Philosophical Society* was most helpful. The Minutes of the Society, the Archives, the Treasurers' Records, etc., provided the skeleton for the history of these furnishings. The physical descriptions of the items themselves were made by David Borodin, of Frisk and Borodin Appraisers, Ltd., outstanding authorities on furniture. I have relied, wherever possible, on the memoirs published by the Society for a descriptive note of the members who owned, or in whose memory, the furniture listed herein was presented.

I am indebted to Dr. Herman H. Goldstine, Executive Officer of the Society, for asking me to prepare this manuscript for publication. The Staff of the Society, especially Carole Le Faivre, have been unusually helpful and I thank them for their help. Frank Margeson, photographer for the Library, provided the excellent reproductions included here. Richard Ahlborn, Smithsonian Institution, and Dr. Isadora Rose-de Viejo, Associate Curator of Sculpture and Decorative Arts of the Hispanic Society of America, provided much of the material used in the description of the Spanish-type armchair. Roger Moss, Director of The Athenaeum of Philadelphia, gave generously of his time while I was researching the history of the Joseph Bonaparte chair. I am deeply grateful for the interest and help Dr. Silvio Bedini, Keeper of Rare Books, National Museum of American History, Smithsonian Institution, gave me. His insight and penetrating questions improved the manuscript considerably.

Most of all, however, I wish to thank David Borodin for his unfailing help and interest over the years and his concise descriptions of the articles listed in this volume.

The American Philosophical Society

The American Philosophical Society held in Philadelphia for promoting useful knowledge was founded in 1743 by Benjamin Franklin and his friends. It is the oldest learned society in the United States. Its home, Philosophical Hall, stands on Independence Square and its library is across Fifth Street from the Hall. Both buildings are in, but not of, Independence National Historical Park. The Society originally rented rooms for meetings, but while Philosophical Hall was being erected, it met in President Benjamin Franklin's home. Since 1789 it has met in Philosophical Hall. For well over a century the Society used only the second-floor rooms on the south side for itself. The rest of the building was rented. Subsequently, the Society occupied the entire building.

Since the Society is a scientific and practical Society, it never tried to collect antiques, *per se*. The archives of the Society are wonderfully complete, but there are few entries in them referring to furnishings of the eighteenth-century chambers. The Society had no money for purchasing furniture when it moved into Philosophical Hall. Indeed, it borrowed $500 from President Franklin to roof the building. Probably benches were made for the use of the members by carpenters who worked on the construction of the Hall. Benches had been used in the rented quarters, for an entry in the Minutes of 27 February 1786[1] records that benches had been brought in for such a meeting. All expenditures were carefully noted in the Treasurer's Records, so each purchase of furnishings for the first century of using

Philosophical Hall are fairly easy to note. Items wore out and were replaced, so a listing of the various purchases shows the use made of various articles deemed necessary for furnishings.

Since bookcases were essential for storing the growing library of the Society, cases must have been built into the walls by the carpenters before the Society moved into the Hall. After a few years, on 21 April 1803, carpenter William Broom and painter J. Carter were paid $77.36 for "Secretary's case and glass upper part," no doubt used for additional book shelving. A mahogany bookcase was purchased for $22 on 31 December 1804 at the sales by York and Lippincott. Additional bookcases were made by carpenter William Broom on 27 June 1805, costing $26.80. On 3 December 1815 Thomas Parker and William Broom were paid $101.31 for "Bookcases & Sundry work." Carpenter Broom was paid $177.03 in 1824 for "book case over w[est] windows" and sundry other work. Another bookcase was purchased from J. McClure for $66.43 on 26 October 1843.

An oilcloth rug costing $2.25 was purchased 31 December 1814 for use before the fire-place. Another "floor cloth" was acquired from the same dealer, Isaac McCauly, on 14 February 1828. By 1836 the Society purchased a carpet from Mr. Lapley for $56.38.

Since the mineral collection was growing rapidly, carpenters made mineral cases and by 4 November 1803 J. Carter and George Flake were paid $50.20 for "painting and glazing one case."[2]

In 1816 a "large case was made for the Muhlenberg herbarium," as were a closet and three "tables very strong," costing $52.54. Later in the year a large case was made "in the corner for the transit instrument" at a cost of $47.85.[3]

In December 1828, Kappa Lamba fraternity began renting rooms for "meetings 2nd & 4th Wednesday of each month." On 27 October 1834 the Society purchased "Settees, chairs, table &c." for $20 from the fraternity.[4]

By 1830 the members decided to spend $500 for "the alterations of & furnishing the Society's Room." Carpenter David Lapsley was paid $130.15 for furniture later in the year. John Kenworthy earned $1.50 on 17 December 1830 for "Staining washboard and 2 Tables." The next year Mr. Sykes was given $100 "for furniture of S[outh] E[ast] room" and Mr. Stewart earned $20 for "alterations Hall furniture." Also in 1831 the Society paid $35 for a "table in the Hall of the Society."

A "Mineral case & Table of Society" cost $170.05 in 1838, and "three chairs" were acquired from employee William Warren.[5] Following John Vaughan's death in 1841, the Society purchased some furniture for $50 which William Warren inherited from Vaughan.[6]

On 27 January 1843 a "Lecturer's Desk for Lecture Room" was purchased from William McGuiyson for $7. "One counting hous-desk" was bought from D. K. Large on 27 February 1844. Another counting house desk, mahogany this time, was purchased from W. M'Ilvaine for $20 on 2 March 1847. On 23 April of that year a stool was purchased from Mr. McDonough for $2.50.[7]

Other items acquired by the Society are described individually in this volume.

The only non-commercial furnishings the Society owns express its interest in famous members of the Society, and generally, only in the most outstanding and active members who contributed significantly to the meetings, *Transactions* and *Proceedings*, and members whose memory was held most dear. The limited funds of the Society were expended, for the most part, on its publications, the upkeep of Philosophical Hall, the acquisition of portraits and busts of its former presidents or great men, the management and care of its Cabinet of Curiosities, and the library.

Over the years, to 1887, valuable pieces of furniture were acquired through purchase and gift. The inertia of years has elevated some of these into the status of antiques, and they continue to be used today.

Astronomical Timepiece

The Society's first major undertaking was to cooperate with the Royal Society of London in observing the transit of Venus of 1769. Later in the year, the Society determined to make observations of the transit of Mercury and ordered William Smith and John Ewing to arrange with Edward Duffield, who was also a member of the Society, to have an astronomical timepiece constructed "in a plain & cheap manner." The report of the committee was that Duffield would make a timepiece "and has it in such forwardness that he expects to have it ready for observing the ensuing transit." Three weeks later the clock was reported finished and ready for use.[8] The *Transactions* records the use of the clock at the Society's observatory in Independence Square 9 November 1769:

> Still having the same instruments in our Observatory . . . together with a new

Time-Piece made by Mr. *Duffield*, of this city, with an ingenious contrivance of his, in the construction of the pendulum, to remedy the irregularities arising from heat and cold; we paid the utmost attention to the going of the clock, both before and after the transit.[9]

In February of the following year Duffield was paid £15.17.6 for the timepiece. The committee appointed to examine the timepiece and recommend payment thought "the work good & the charge reasonable."[10]

The movement of this Chippendale mahogany tall-case astronomical clock was made by Edward Duffield and is housed in a Philadelphia case, ca. 1770. The bell-top hood has an arched crest resembling thorny branches which center three wooden beet-shape finials over a deep molded cornice. A square glazed face-door with column corners opens to a silvered brass 12½″ dial of black enameled Roman and Arabic numerals in hour and minute rings respectively. The hour and minute hands and a sunk second dial are above the keyhole. The inscription of the maker is: "Duffield, Phila." The waisted case below has a molded, hinged door above a molded base on shallow bracket feet. A conventional train time of four arbors and a dead-beat escapement (located between the plates) form the movement. There is an eight-pound pendulum with a pine rod and lens-shaped bob which is driven by a crutch wire. It is adjustable but not compensated. The height is 99″; the width is 23½″; and the depth is 10½″.[11]

Although the maker of the case is unknown, Benjamin Randolph had done work for Duffield during the period and perhaps he made it.

Fig. 1. Duffield Astronomical Timepiece

President's Desk

There is a reference that the "President's table" or "desk" was acquired in 1838.[12] It must have been made by a joiner/carpenter. In the photographs of ca. 1884 in the library, the Franklin library chair, once the "President's Chair," is clearly depicted behind this article of furniture, now also in the library. It was removed from Philosophical Hall in 1975. During the last half-century it had been known as a lectern. It is a low, oblong, rectangular case hinged to the front with four frame-and-panel doors opening to interiors 15" deep. The center cabinet is 36¾" wide and 22½" high and has two shelves. The two side cabinets are 15" wide and 22½" high with no shelves. They are surrounded by conformingly paneled sides above a continuous plain base molding, painted white overall and fitted with an overhanging oblong top of composition board with rounded corners. Overall the desk is 84" long, 36" wide, and 30¾" high. The top has been rebuilt, possibly in 1947 when Philosophical Hall was restored. The rear is open for chairs and legs.[13]

Fig. 2. *President's Desk*

Fig. 3. Bookcases

Bookcases

White painted hardwood and glass library bookcases were made in 1843 by J. McClure of Philadelphia for the Society.[14] They lined the walls of the apartments of the Society on the second floor of Philosophical Hall. They have pairs of hinged double-panel glazed cabinet doors enclosing wooden shelves beneath a plain cyma-recta molded cornice. They are finished with a plain, shallow base molding. When Philosophical Hall was completely remodeled in 1947 a few of these bookcases were retained. They have no distinctive features: they were made by a joiner/carpenter for a utilitarian function and they continue to be so utilized. McClure was paid $66.43 on 26 October 1843 for his work.[15]

Partners Desk (Fig. 4)

In 1872 the Society purchased a partners desk for the library from the Philadelphia firm of Walton, Lippincott and Scott for $168.[16] It is a Victorian walnut partners desk which was made by Walter and Scott, Philadelphia cabinet-makers on South Second Street, Philadelphia. It has an overhanging, rectangular top with molded edge, notched corners and a composition-inset surface above a symmetrical arrangement of five drawers on each side. These are flanked by chamfered corners on massive fluted octagonal legs, turned with compressed bulbous collars, ankles and feet. Its height is 31½"; its width is 59"; and its depth is 38".[17]

In July 1978 this desk was in "a deplorable state" and was extensively rebuilt, restored and refinished by Mervin B. Marvin. All drawers and slides were rebuilt, the molding at the kneehole was restored, and it was refinished.[18]

Fig. 4. Partners Desk

Settees, and Chairs and a Pennsylvania Kitchen Table

The Society purchased, 1 November 1875, settees (Fig. 5) and chairs and a Pennsylvania kitchen table (Fig. 6) for its rooms from the Philadelphia furniture manufacturers and upholsterers, William Smith and Richard R. Campion on South Third Street in Philadelphia.[19] Four of the settees and thirty-four of the chairs are still in use. Each item of this American, late-Victorian caned walnut furniture has a crescent-shaped open domical crestrail, centered with an incised tablet surmounted with a bar-form crest. The crest is above a caned back-panel shaped to bottom above a three-way bulbous stretcher conjoining the fluted square stiles. The grooved arms with scrolled handholds are raised on shaped supports on a caned seat with bowed front above ringed and tapered turned round legs conjoined by double vasiform front-stretchers and double plain round side-stretchers. The chairs are 38½" high, 22½" wide, and the depth is 21". The settees are 43" high, 72" wide and 21" deep.[20]

This furniture is a great favorite with the members and it receives heavy wear during the biannual meetings of

Fig. 5a. Settee

Fig. 5b. Detail of Settee

the Society. The caning must constantly be redone. These and the Pennsylvania kitchen table cost $578.[21]

The Pennsylvania kitchen table is American Victorian in style and is of walnut. It has an overhanging rectangular top with inset surface and molded front edge above a shallow, straight apron fitted to front with two wide shallow drawers. The drawers have brass scoop-type grips and are flanked by protruding square corners applied with renaissance-style fluted strapwork brackets with bosses. These are raised on massive tapered round legs, ring-turned with compressed bulbous sections and caster feet. Some of the brasses have been replaced. One end of the table is squared where a shorter table could abut: the other end has rounded corners. The height is 30", the width is 96", and the depth is 48".[22]

Fig. 6a. Chair

Fig. 6b. Pennsylvania Kitchen Table

Fig. 7. Secretary Table

Secretary Table

A table, known as the Secretary's table, is in the Hall. Former curator, Edgar P. Richardson, noted that: "The library tables made by a joiner-turner for the Library Company of Philadelphia in 1740 are earlier examples of this type."[23] It is an American Chippendale stained pine and maple (or oak) piece and was made in Philadelphia in the early nineteenth century. It has a plain overhanging rectangular top above a molded straight apron which is fitted at each end with a thumb molded drawer with brass pulls and keyholes. It stands on ringed round legs which are conjoined at the block-form ankles with a molded block stretcher above short rounded feet of tear-drop shape. It is 29¾" high; it is 59" long; and, it is 34½" wide.[24]

The only reference located for this item is a note in the Treasurer's Records for 1838: "Table for Secretaries. $28.00."[25]

1. American Philosophical Society (hereafter APS). Minutes, 27 Feb. 1786 (hereafter Min.).
2. APS. Treasurer's Records, 1803–1836 (hereafter Treas. Recs.).
3. APS. Archives (hereafter Archives). Account of repairs . . . , 1816–1820.
4. Ibid., Papers pertaining to furnishings . . . , 27 Oct. 1834–21 Apr. 1847.
5. Treas. Recs., 1830–1841.
6. Archives. Papers pertaining to furnishings . . . , 27 Oct. 1834–21 Apr. 1847.
7. Treas. Recs., 1843–1847.
8. Min., 15 Sept. and 6 Oct. 1769.
9. "An Account of the Transit of Mercury over the Sun, on November 9th, 1769, N.S.," *Transactions of the American Philosophical Society* (1771), 1:82–88. Hereafter referred to as: *Trans.*
10. Min., 2 Feb. 1770.
11. David Borodin, "Physical descriptions of antiques in the American Philosophical Society," 1985 (hereafter Borodin). Robert P. Multhauf, *A Catalogue of Instruments and Models in the Possession of the American Philosophical Society, Memoirs of the American Philosophical Society* (1961), 53:49–50 (hereafter *Cat. of Insts.*).
12. Treas. Recs., 1838.
13. Borodin.
14. Treas. Recs., 1843.
15. Borodin.
16. Treas. Recs., 13 March 1872.
17. Borodin.
18. APS. Edgar P. Richardson, Curator (hereafter Richardson).
19. Treas. Recs., 1875.
20. Borodin.
21. Treas. Recs., 1875.
22. Borodin.
23. Richardson.
24. Borodin.
25. Treas. Recs., 1838.

Benjamin Franklin
Secretary 1743; President 1769–1790

The two giants of the Society are Benjamin Franklin and Thomas Jefferson, each so famous that they need no introduction.

The Society began when Franklin published and mailed out a "Proposal for promoting useful knowledge among the *British Plantations* in America." He offered himself as secretary "'till they shall be provided with one more capable." Not only was Franklin active in founding the Society, he was its first president. As president, he continually helped the infant Society while he was in England and France, forwarding publications and gifts, introducing people, and suggesting new members. Upon his return from France in 1785 he acted as president until his death in 1790. Due to his ill health which caused him great pain in moving about, many meetings were held in his home. Thus the Society did not have to pay rent for a meeting place.

Franklin was the most famous scientist of the United States. His work on electricity had catapulted him into instant fame in Europe and his further scientific work was admired. He published eight articles in the Society's *Transactions* (vols. 2 and 3): the most noted of these is his study of the Gulf Stream which was done with the aid of a nephew, Jonathan Williams. Other articles concerned causes and cures of smokey chimneys; a new stove for burning pit coal; hygrometers; the formation of the earth; light and heat; magnetism; and a process for making large sheets of paper in the Chinese manner.

There are many likenesses of Franklin in Philosophical Hall and one is the first oil portrait acquired by the Society. It was painted in 1772 by Charles Willson Peale after the 1767 portrait by David Martin. Peale presented it to the Society 16 December 1785 and the members, after expressing their thanks, asked Peale to retain it until the proposed Philosophical Hall was built. Another portrait is by, or attributed to, Charles Amedée Philippe Van Loo, and there are four busts of Franklin after Jean Jacques Caffière and Jean Antoine Houdon.[1]

President's Chair (Fig. 8a, b)

The first known article of furniture the Society acquired as a keepsake was the chair which Franklin bought, and perhaps designed, for his library. When, aged and ill, he returned to Philadelphia from France in 1784, he settled into his house—already filled with his daughter's growing family. He built a room for his books onto the house, though he knew he could not justify such an addition, admitting that age would soon "oblige me to quit it." He had three unusual chairs in this library: one was a "Fan Chair" on rockers which stirred the air over him when he rocked. Another, a "Library chair," was later given to David Hosack by Franklin's granddaughter, Catherine Bache, and Hosack presented it to the Literary and Philosophical Society of New York.[2] The third was used by Franklin when he presided and the American Philosophical Society met in his house to honor him and to keep him from having to move about. After his death, the members asked his family for this library chair and Richard Bache, Franklin's son-in-law, presented it on 2 February 1792.[3]

This venerable Chippendale mahogany, open-arm library chair, upholstered in leather, was made in Philadelphia ca. 1760–1780. It has a tall, upholstered back with a serpentine crest which is flanked by upholstered, shaped arms. The arms are raised on concave supports above an upholstered seat which has a deeply aproned seat rail. The seat lifts up, exposing two attached steps forming a stool which enabled the user to reach higher shelves. The chair is raised on molded square front legs and flaring square back legs, all on casters. They are conjoined by an H-stretcher. The chair has its original leather, which has been strengthened. The height is 50"; the seat is 18"; the width is 27½"; and the depth is 34¼".[4]

Since Franklin was president of the Society from 1769 until his death, the members called this chair the "President's Chair" and it was used by the various presidents from the time it was received until 1931. It was "retired" when Francis Xavier Dercum died in it, while presiding at the meeting of 24 April 1931.[5]

Fig. 8a. Franklin's Chair (closed)

Fig. 8b. Franklin's Chair (open)

Tall-Case Timepiece
(Grandmother) (Fig. 9)

During the 1930s the Society considered the purchase of a tall-case clock for Philosophical Hall. It was decided 4 June 1935 that one would not be purchased unless it had a historical association.[6] A timepiece which fulfilled this requirement was presented by Junius S. and Henry S. Morgan in 1954.

President Owen J. Roberts learned that the Morgan brothers wished to donate this timepiece, so he wrote Junius S. Morgan on 6 July 1954 that the Society would be delighted to have it and would "like very much to place this clock in our Hall." Morgan replied 8 July 1954 that his brother and he would "be very glad to give it." Neither he nor his brother knew much about it except "my father acquired the clock a good many years ago but neither my brother nor I have any particular knowledge as to his purchase of it. We both feel, however, that it should be among the mementos of Benjamin Franklin that your Society has."

By 10 August 1954 the timepiece had been received and was in Philosophical Hall. J. S. Morgan was notified that when "the Executive Committee is able to meet in September it will be determined where the clock is to be placed in the Hall, and will at that time have an expert clock man assemble it and set it up."

The Society sent "hearty thanks" to the two Morgans on 23 November 1954. The clock, by this date, was in good running order and "has been of the greatest interest to the members who attended the Autumn Meeting."[7]

This clock, reputedly, was once

Fig. 9. Grandmother Timepiece

owned by Franklin and had descended through the Bache family. It was exhibited during the 1870s or thereabouts in the Yale University Library where it was listed as a "Franklin clock." Brass plates on the clock stated that the owners were Benjamin Franklin, died 1790; Benjamin Franklin Bache, died 1798; Hartman Bache, died 1872; Richard Meade Bache, died 1907; and René Bache, who died in 1933 when the Morgans purchased it.

It is an elegant Queen Anne mahogany tall-case (grandmother) clock with movement by Edward Duffield of Philadelphia, made ca. 1750. Both the case and dial top are highly decorated. The movement is conventional, containing four arbors in the time train of movement and a recoil escapement. A circle for the days of the month runs in three grooved wheels behind the dial and a wooden pendulum rod (not the original) is driven by a crutch wire. The Philadelphia case has a bell-top hood surmounted with wood finials, spool-turned in form, above a delicate blind-carved frieze of acanthus molding. This molding and a stepped cyma-molded cornice are over a bold extrados molding which encloses a column-cornered domical glazed face-door. The brass dial, inscribed "Edw. Duffield, Philadelphia," has gilt scrollwork spandrels, each of which has a profile wearing a feathered headdress. Black enameled Roman and Arabic numerals are in hour and minute rings respectively and there is a sunk seconds dial above a keyhole and a date register. At the top of the dial is a lunette with moon sphere in silver and black with a short cylinder which shows the number of days of the age of the moon. The waisted case beneath has a molded trunk-door with a domical top. The base

is plain molded and raised on shallow bracket feet. The case is 82½" high; it is 16" wide; and it is 9½" deep.[8]

The inventory of Franklin's estate lists: "Time piece in library 7.10.0" which might refer to this item.

Tall-Case Timepiece (Fig. 10)

Another Duffield clock was listed in Franklin's estate inventory as "Clock (on the stairs) 20.0.0." This may have been the one purchased from a Franklin descendant, Mrs. Henrietta Bache Jayne, in 1961. It is a superb Philadelphia walnut tall-case clock with movement by Edward Duffield, constructed ca. 1775. Reputedly, it was owned by Franklin and descended through the Bache family.

The mechanism is the eight day weight drive type having a bell strike and seconds beat pendulum. The brass clockworks plates have four bulbous turned pillars with rings and are of a construction that could be considered heavier and thicker than many early American or Colonial American clocks. There is no falseplate connecting the mechanism with the dial. The strike mechanism is the rack and snail type, setting the clock to strike the number of hours on the hour only. The escapement is the anchor recoil type.[9]

The case has a hood with molded swan's neck cresting, terminating in leafy rosettes. It is flanked and centered with carved wooden finials in the form of flaming urns above a bold extrados-molding, enclosing a column-cornered domical glazed face-door. The brass dial contains scrollwork spandrels and black enameled Roman and Arabic numerals in hour and minute rings respectively. There is a sunk seconds dial above two keyholes and date register, all beneath a lunette centered with a circu-

lar brass boss inscribed "Edw. Duffield
Philadelphia." The waisted case beneath has carved, fluted, quarter column
corners which flank a hinged molded
trunk-door of fine grain, shaped to the
top. The base has conforming corners
and molded panel above a stepped
molding which is raised on shaped,
ogival bracket feet. The case is 104″
high, 21½″ wide and 11″ deep.[10]

    Although the case maker is un-
known, Benjamin Randolph did work
for Duffield and he may have made the
case.

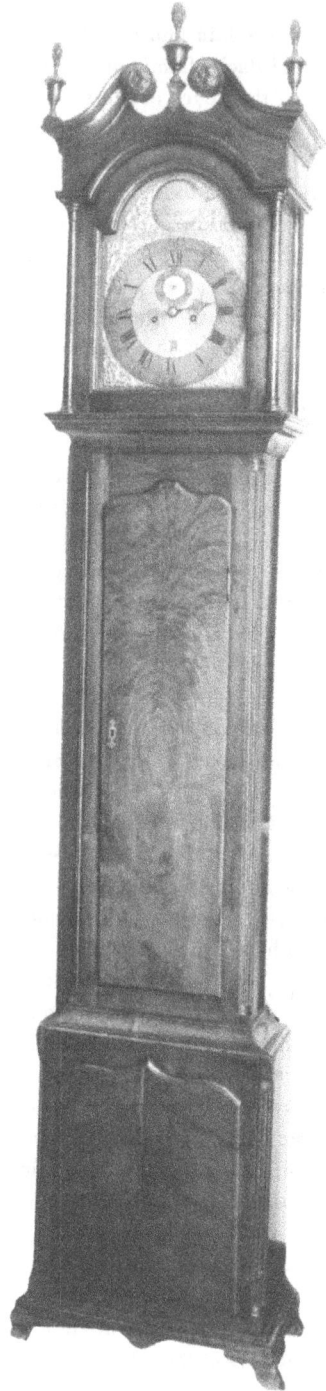

Fig. 10. Tall-Case Timepiece

Chess Sets (Fig. 11)

The fascinating game of chess, "the most universal game known among men," probably originated in India in the sixth and seventh centuries. It spread to Persia and then to the Levant and possibly was introduced to Europe by the Muslims. By the thirteenth century it had undergone little change from the game the Persians played, and was enjoyed all over Europe. There is an extensive literature on the subject and Franklin, who greatly enjoyed the game, playing it with friends in Philadelphia, London and Paris, added a short article concerning its virtues: "The Morals of Chess" (1774). He wrote these "Morals" to help "correct (among a few young friends) some little improprieties in the practice" of the game.[11] Imagery derived from the game can be found throughout Franklin's writings. The Society owns two sets of chessmen which once belonged to Franklin: a large one and a

tiny traveling set. Both are probably French in origin. The large set descended through the Duane family and the pedigree is excellent. William Duane (1760–1835) and Benjamin Franklin Bache edited the Philadelphia newspaper, *Aurora*. Duane's son, William John Duane, married Deborah Bache, a granddaughter of Franklin, Their son, William Duane (1807–1882), stated "repeatedly" that the set belonged originally to Franklin. The set was presented to Russell Duane (1866–1938) in 1878 by William Duane and subsequently it was inherited by the son of Russell Duane, Morris Duane, in 1939. Morris Duane, who was a member of the Society, presented it on 28 December 1976.

I think it is interesting to note that when I first got these Chessmen from my father they were contained in an old wooden box with a sliding wooden top, which my wife, thinking that an item of such value should be contained in something better than an old wooden box, threw away. In addition, there was an old Chess Board but my recollection is

Fig. 11a. Chess Set (large)

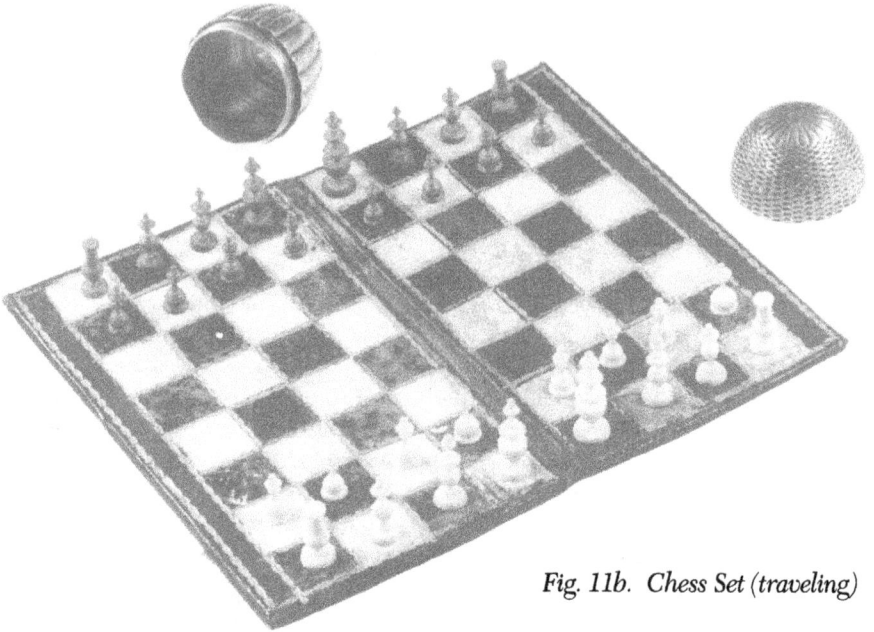

Fig. 11b. Chess Set (traveling)

CHESS SET (traveling)

that my father told me that while it was a very old Board he did not think it belonged to Benjamin Franklin, although the Chessmen in the original box did.[12]

This fruitwood chess set, probably pearwood, was made in France ca. 1750–1780. In French sets of that period the knights have a most distinctive form: the top disc is sliced on two sides to form a point "a shape somewhat resembling a hat of the period" rather than the head of a horse.

The Encyclopedia of Diderot and D'Alembert, the first parts of which appeared in 1750, has an article on chess, and its engraving of chess pieces shows the Knight of this abstract kind, without the horse's head that had been used in earlier times, and later.

And in the Carnavelet Museum in Paris, among other historical exhibits of the Revolution, is the chess game used by the Royal Family when held prisoners in the Temple, awaiting trial. These, too, are of pearwood and are very like the Franklin chessmen in size and character.[13]

The size of the kings is 9 cm. and the colors of the men are black and white. The chessboard, never the property of Franklin, is of English manufacture of the nineteenth century and is of paper. It is 42¾ cm. square with a red outer cover enfolding black and white squares with a red trim. The board was presented by John Harbeson in 1977.

The small, traveling chess set was presented by Frances Margaret Bradford July 1960. She was a descendant of Mary Stevenson Hewson, the young friend of Franklin whom he called Polly and whom he helped educate while living at her mother's house in London during the 1750–1760s. Franklin's correspondence with her is charming, especially the "Craven Street Gazette" (written in the style of the popular gazettes of the day, but referring to Franklin's household activities). He wrote this "Gazette" possibly to amuse the young girl and to keep her attention focused on home while she was away in school. This correspondence was acquired from Miss Bradford in 1956. Mrs. Hewson emigrated to the United States in 1786 after visiting Franklin in France. Perhaps the set was presented by Franklin to her shortly before her emigration.

This set of chessmen is of ivory and the men are red and white. The kings are 1¾ cm. high and all pieces are contained in a threaded, silver, egg-shaped, grooved container 4 cm. long. The board is folded, with a red leather gold-tooled cover, and the black and white leather squares on the inner side have a red leather trim with gold tooling. The board is 11½ cm. by 9¾ cm.

1. *A Catalogue of Portraits and Other Works of Art in the Possession of the American Philosophical Society*, 26–41; *Memoirs of the American Philosophical Society* (1961), 54 (hereafter *Cat. of Portraits*).

2. "Armchair from Benjamin Franklin's Library." See David Hosack microfilm in the APS. Papers, 1797–1826, no. 7.

3. Min., 3 Feb. 1792.

4. Borodin.

5. Charles W. Burr, "Memoir of Dr. Francis X. Dercum," reprinted from *Medical Life*, April 1932, 8.

6. APS. Committee on Hall. Minutes, 10 June 1935.

7. APS. Archives. Owen J. Roberts to J. S. Morgan, 6 July 1954: J. S. Morgan to O. J. Roberts, 8 July 1954; O. J. Roberts to J. S. Morgan, 10 Aug. 1954; Ibid., 23 Nov. 1954.

8. Borodin; and *Cat. of Insts.*, 50–51.

9. Gordon S. Converse, "Descriptive Notes on the Clock made by Edward Duffield at the American Philosophical Society, 1986."

10. Borodin.

11. Franklin, Benjamin. Morals of Chess. 1774.

12. Archives. Legal Papers. Morris Duane to APS; 28 Dec. 1976.

13. Ibid. John Harbeson to Morris Duane, 29 Nov. 1951.

14. These two chess sets have been written up by Robert R. Radcliff; "Franklin's Chessmen Were as Practical and Sturdy as Old Ben Himself," *Chess Life*, June 1986, pp. 386–87.

John Bartram
Original Member

John Bartram was America's best known naturalist of the late eighteenth century and its first native botanist. He, along with Franklin, worked to establish the American Philosophical Society and to keep it alive. Both enjoyed chess and perhaps they played with the same set which was presented to the Society on 17 January 1968 by John Harbeson, noted collector of chessmen. With this set is a contemporary chessboard.

This gift is "believed to have been John Bartram's" and it was acquired by Harbeson from American Philosophical Society President Julian Boyd. Boyd did

not recall from whom he obtained it, although he does remember some other circumstances, especially that it was at a meeting of the Numismatic and Anti-

quarian Society [of Philadelphia] that he showed you [Harbeson] some of the pieces and, when he saw your keen interest in them, offered them to you.[1]

It seems most appropriate that this chess set was presented on Franklin's birthday.

The set is contained in a contemporary walnut box 28 cm. long, 15½ cm. wide and 10½ cm. deep (Fig. 12). There is a label pasted on the inside of the lid containing manuscript notations: "John Bartram. Price [indecipherable]." The box contains a complete set of black and natural wood chessmen, although two pawns are later replacements: they are much smaller, and one is crudely carved.

The pine chessboard, deeply cracked and split in the center, is inlaid with alternating grained squares of wood. It is 47 cm. by 37¾ cm.

1. APS. Archives. Librarians' Records: W. J. Bell, Jr., to John Harbeson, 22 Jan. 1968.

Fig. 12. John Bartram Chess Set

David Rittenhouse
President of the Society 1791–1796

Astronomical Timepiece (Fig. 13)

Rittenhouse was born in Germantown, Pennsylvania, and spent the early part of his life on a farm. His plough, the fences, the stones of the fields, etc., were covered with figures which demonstrated his talent for mathematical studies. Since he was physically weak, his parents agreed that he learn the trade of a clock and mathematical instrument maker, and he taught himself. Interested in the principles of natural philosophy, he mastered Sir Isaac Newton's *Principia*. Rittenhouse developed the science of fluxions, and thought he invented it, but later he learned of the contest between Newton and Leibnitz for the honor of the discovery. Before he moved to Philadelphia and while he was constructing instruments, he executed an orrery, now at Princeton University, representing the revolutions of the heavenly bodies.

He moved into Philadelphia in 1770 and continued his trade of instrument and clock maker. He was one of the original members of the Society when it was united with the American Society in 1769.

The Royal Society of London asked as many colonials as could to observe the transit of Venus in 1769. The Society agreed to participate and Rittenhouse was one of a committee chosen to do so. He made his own astronomical transit telescope (now in the possession of the Society) and an astronomical clock. His observations of this transit were published by the Society in its *Transactions* and were received with great satisfaction by the astronomers of Europe.

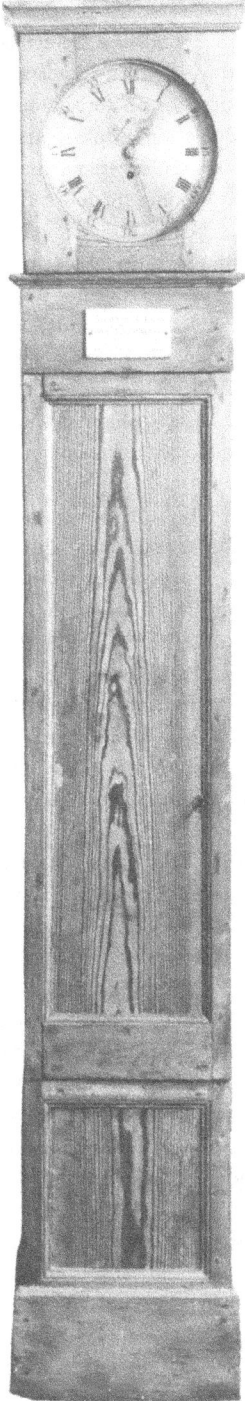

Fig. 13. Astronomical Timepiece

He continued to publish in the *Transactions* and his works were universally praised. He assisted in determining the length of five degrees of longitude from a point in the Delaware River in order to fix the western limits of Pennsylvania in 1786. He assisted, also, in fixing the boundaries of New Jersey and Massachusetts.[1]

Rittenhouse was an active member of the Society and succeeded Franklin as president. He bequeathed his observatory (located at 7th and Arch Streets in Philadelphia) to the Society, but Philadelphia grew so rapidly that Rittenhouse's heirs proposed on 30 March 1810 that the observatory be returned to them, since it was now surrounded by buildings and could not be used for its original purpose. "The transit instrument and the clock we shall present to your Society and you will also be desired to accept the money bequeathed by our mother [$200] to keep the building in repair."[2]

The Society considered this request of the Rittenhouse daughters and formed a committee which reported favorably on it and the Society agreed to it. The timepiece was in the observatory with the transit telescope when the property was reconveyed to the family 16 November 1810 and a committee was appointed to move the instruments. The Society "authorized to invite Mr. [Andrew] Ellicott to assist, and to pay his expenses."[3] Ellicott was paid $70 for this work and for repairing the "Transit Instrument."[4] The fund Mrs. Rittenhouse bequeathed for "the purpose of raising an annual fund to be applied to the keeping of the observatory clock in order" still produces interest and is still used.

Even though the timepiece was regarded as excellent, it seems never to have been used again for astronomical purposes. Benjamin Smith Barton described it as "an excellent timepiece, having for its pendulum rod a flat steel bar, and a bob weighing about 12 pounds, and vibrating in a small arc. This went eight days, did not stop when wound up, beat dead seconds, and was kept in motion by a weight of 5 pounds."[5]

The transit telescope, however, was used for some time and even loaned, but no record of such use of the timepiece exists.

By 1818 the Rittenhouse pieces were obsolete for astronomical purposes and when the Society proposed building an observatory in Philadelphia's Center Square, Secretary John Vaughan wrote John Sargeant and Joseph Hopkinson asking for "astron. inst. for our Obser-[vator]y." He asked specifically for a transit instrument, an astronomical clock, a reflecting circle and an acromatic telescope.[6]

On 9 March 1835 Thomas Voight was asked to clean the clock[7] and he was paid $3 on 1 April.[8] On 19 March 1869 the members asked the curators to confer on the Rittenhouse clock, with power to act. They had it cleaned by "proper hands" 2 April 1869. On 16 April, even though the clock was no longer fit as an astronomical timepiece, the "Curators were authorized to have the Rittenhouse Clock put into complete order as an 8 day clock, to preserve its identity, although it can no longer be of service for astronomical purposes."

And on 20 May 1870 the Society authorized the payment of $12 to Mr. Gropengieser "for keeping Rittenhouse clock in order for one year."[9]

DAVID RITTENHOUSE

The cat gut which held "the weight of the Rittenhouse clock" broke in August 1907 and the weight fell, breaking "the glass compensating tube holding the mercury" and detaching the pendulum.[10] On 2 December "J. C. Caldwell & Co. repaired the Rittenhouse Clock. . . . they agreed to place a glass diaphram [sic] in front of the pendulum, and between it and the weight, so that, in case of breakage of the cord, the weight cannot strike the pendulum and break it."[11]

Shortly thereafter the clock was not in good condition and it was repaired by Riggs for $8 on 3 March 1914. Later, 16 November 1820, Secretary I. M. Hays reported that the clock "has never been fixed, nor, so far as I know has the clock maker ever been paid for his work on it. . . . I will try to get the clock going, as we rather take pride in the fact that notwithstanding its age it is a going clock which keeps good time and in its present condition we cannot make this assertion."[12]

Robert P. Multhauf described the movement of the timepiece as having

heavy brass plates with a pillar at each of the four corners contain[ing] the deadbeat escapement and going train of two many-toothed wheels. The motion work is between the dial and front plate. A small gear on the #2 gear arbor drives a large gear carrying the minute hand. The hour hand is driven by the latter gear through a compound idler gear and pinion. The second hand is mounted on the escape wheel arbor. The pendulum vibrates seconds and is mercury compensated. It is in two pieces connected by a yoke, and suspended by two springs. A thermometer is mounted on the back of the case.[13]

The case of this astronomical clock is pine. The hood has a plain cyma-molded cornice above a circular-windowed hinged face-door which opens to a 10⅝" diameter dial which is probably of cold silvered brass. The straight plain case below is fitted with a recess-paneled trunk-door above a conforming panel over the deep plain base. The height is 83½"; the width is 13¼"; and the depth is 9½".[14]

Rittenhouse's portrait, by Charles Willson Peale, was ordered by the Society in 1791, the year of his election to the presidency. It was the second portrait, after that of Franklin (also by Charles Willson Peale), to be hung in Philosophical Hall. In 1795 the Italian idealist, Giuseppe Ceracchi, presented a marble bust which he had carved of his friend Rittenhouse. Rittenhouse and Ceracchi had searched vainly for an American marble quarry to equal that of Carrara and other Italian marbles.[15]

1. Benjamin Rush, *Eulogium Intended to Perpetuate the Memory of the Late David Rittenhouse, late President of the American Philosophical Society Delivered before the Society in the First Presbyterian Church, in High-Street, Philadelphia, on the 17th December 1796* (Philadelphia, [1796]).
2. Archives. Mrs. Sergeant and Mrs. Waters to APS; 30 March 1810; and, Min., 6 April 1810.
3. Min., 16 Nov. 1810.
4. Treas. Recs., 1810.
5. William Barton, *Memoirs of the Life of David Rittenhouse . . . Interspersed with Various Notices of Many Distinguished Men* (Philadelphia: Parker: 1813), 171–72.
6. Archives. John Vaughan to John Sargeant and Joseph Hopkinson, 1818.
7. Min., 9 March 1835; 19 March, 2 April, 16 April 1869; 20 May 1870.
8. Archives. APS. Receipt . . . ; 1 April 1835.
9. Min., 19 March, 2 April, 16 April 1869; 20 May 1870.
10. Archives 5, B, 2. I. M. Hays to C. L. Doolittle; 6 Aug. 1907.
11. Ibid., 2 Dec. 1907.
12. Ibid., 16 Nov. 1920.
13. *Cat. of Insts.*, 49.
14. Borodin.
15. *Cat. of Portraits*, 82–84.

David Steuart Erskine
11th Earl of Buchan
Member 1794

Secretary's Writing Box

Buchan was a well-educated Scottish lord who was interested in many subjects: he contributed to literary publications and wrote biographies and essays. He loved the United States and claimed a relationship with George Washington with whom he corresponded. Washington proposed him for membership in the Society in 1794 and he was duly elected that same year.[1]

The earl presented on 5 October 1787 through Walter Minto an engraving of John Napier (or Neper), laird of Merchiston, the inventor of logarithms. It was noted in the donations in the *Transactions* as: "A portrait of Lord Napier, the famous inventor of Logarithms."[2] The print was once elaborately framed and hung for many years in Philosophical Hall where it was exposed to the light and is now badly discolored (Fig. 14).

In 1792 Buchan gave Washington a snuffbox made from the tree which sheltered Sir William Wallace. On 22 April 1793 Washington sent him a map, by James Thackara, of the "Federal City," for Washington never referred to the capital of the United States by name. Buchan presented this map to the Society 16 April 1802: "Plan of the city of Washington in the territory of Columbia, ceded by the states of Virginia and Maryland to the United States of America, and by them established as the seat of their government, after the year MDCCC."[3]

On 17 January 1795 the earl presented a cast of himself done by James Tassie. It is a tiny bas-relief in paste, mounted on marble. Pasted on the back is a label: "To the Philosophical Society of Philadelphia as a testimony of my respect."[4] Additional evidence of his "respect" was soon coming. On 15 May 1795 an unusual box was received from Buchan and the Minutes read:

> An authentic picture of Copernicus on the lid of a box of Yew; and on the inside one of Napier; sent by the Earl of Buchan; who consecrates this curious piece of furniture to the Society; desiring however that Dr. Rittenhouse should have the use and custody of it during his life, producing it occasionally when he thinks proper.

The *Transactions* records the gift and the two portraits are listed in the *Catalogue of Portraits*.[5]

The earl's letter presenting this box was addressed to David Rittenhouse on 12 January 1795 from his estate, Dryburgh Abbey, in Scotland:

> My worthy friend Mr. John Millar son of the eminent Professor John Millar of Glasgow whom I recommend to your attention has charged himself with this letter and will deliver to you a writing box which I dedicate to your use as President of the Philosophical Society at Philadelphia & to your Successors in Office as a Testimony of my high esteem for your Literary Character and for that of the Society over which you preside.

> This box is made of Yew, of Black Cherry Tree, Acacia, and Berberry and veneered with Holly all of the growth of my Garden at this place and joined, fitted, & finished by my own Joiner in this House.

> On the lid is an authentic picture of Copernicus, and in the inside thereof is a similar one of Napier. That of Copernicus is from the accurate copy of the Chancellor Hussarzewski's original Picture w[hi]ch was sent by the learned Dr. Wolf of Dantzic to the Royal Society of London & this limning of mine is most faithfully delineated & shaded from a drawing made by Mr. Thomas Parke of Picadilly formerly a pupil of Valentin Green Engraver at London from the Picture in the Royal Society on a Scale proportional in all parts and with great

fidelity, so that I can assure you of my limning being a Facsimile as to the features & countenance.

That of Napier is indeed a most exquisitely beautiful piece by John Brown of Ed[inbu]r[gh] executed with black lead Pencil from an original Portrait in the possession of Lord Napier; & as a drawing with black Lead excells I believe everything of the kind now extant, Mr. Brown having by drawing during Twelve Years in Italy [Footnote: "From Statues"] obtained a supereminent accuracy & beauty of design. I consecrate this interesting piece of Furniture to American Science & to the Philosophical Society of Philadelphia, willing however, that in consideration of the high Esteem I bear to you Personally you should have the custody & use of it, in your own House during your Life, producing it only to the Society for the use of the Secretary when you think proper. I have subjoined by way of Postscript to this letter some particulars related to the residence of Copernicus & his Tomb which I wish you to communicate to our Society. . . .

P.S. Upon the whole it appears that the likeness I send of Copernicus is most to be depended on, and that as such I flatter myself it will be an Heir Loom to Infant America!

Concerning Napier it is needless for me to enlarge—the learned Dr. Minto having enabled me to do justice to his Memory.[6]

Buchan and Minto wrote a life of Napier and published it: a copy was presented to the Society.

LORD JOHN NAPIER

Fig. 14. Secretary's Writing Box

On 16 June 1797 the Minutes record that Mrs. Rittenhouse returned this box to the Society, with the above letter inside.[7] It is a handsome shallow rectangular box of colored woods, somewhat warped today, with the two portraits intact. It is hinged with a lift-lid opening to expose an inset wood tray scooped with ten circular and oblong accessory receptacles. Applied to the lid reverse is a gilt-framed miniature portrait of Napier (in pencil on ivory, by John Brown). The lid exterior-inset at center with a vertical oblong window encloses a portrait of Copernicus (painted by Buchan after Thomas Parke's drawing of the Lorman copy at the Royal Society of London). Its length is 14¾"; its width is 9¾"; and its height is 3¾".[8]

This "writing box" was stored in the attic of Philosophical Hall and forgotten until Henry Phillips, Jr., displayed it and spoke of its history to the members on 20 February 1885.[9]

1. Min., 18 April 1794.
2. Ibid., 5 Oct. 1787; *Trans.*, 3:352.
3. Min., 16 April 1802.
4. *Cat. of Portraits*, 12–13.
5. Min., 15 May 1795; *Trans.* 4:xxiii; *Cat. of Portraits*, 12–13.
6. Archives. D. S. Erskine, Lord Buchan, to D. Rittenhouse, 12 Jan. 1795.
7. Min., 16 June 1797.
8. Borodin.
9. Min., 20 Feb. 1885.

Caspar Wistar
President of the Society
1815–1818

Caspar Wistar was an eminent Philadelphia doctor of German descent. He was only fifteen years old when the Revolution began, and, though his heritage forbad him to fight in it, he helped doctors attend the wounded at the battle of Germantown. Wistar studied medicine under the noted Philadelphia physician, John Redman, and John Jones, an outstanding physician from New York. In 1782 he received the degree of Doctor of Medicine from the University of Pennsylvania and then studied in London and Edinburgh. He was elected president of the Royal Medical Society of Edinburgh due to his "further investigation of natural history." His inaugural dissertation was dedicated to Benjamin Franklin and the famous Scottish physician, William Cullen.

In 1787 he became physician to the Philadelphia Dispensary and in that year he was elected to the College of Physicians of Philadelphia. He labored diligently during the yellow fever epidemics of the late 1790s and caught the dread disease. After recovery he was chosen physician to the Pennsylvania Hospital where he was surgeon. In the same year he became professor of anatomy, midwifery and surgery at the University of Pennsylvania and became sole professor of anatomy in 1808. He was a splendid teacher and used drawings and anatomical models which he provided for the lectures. His *Systems of Anatomy* for students was the first anatomy textbook published in the United States. As a physician he spent much time with each patient better to ascertain the symptoms and be more certain of the disease.

Wistar was elected to membership in the Society in 1787 in recognition of his scientific interests and he became an active member. He served as curator in 1793, in 1795 became vice-president, in 1795 and in 1815 succeeded Jefferson as president. He attended committee meetings assiduously and was an early and strong supporter in opening the Society to the liberal arts.

Corresponding widely with foreign as well as native scientists, Wistar's communications with Thomas Jefferson were the most important. With Jefferson, Wistar developed the science of vertebrate paleontology to such a point that George Gaylord Simpson wrote that they could be called the fathers of that science in America.[1]

Wistar's home was open to men of learning—citizens and strangers alike. Ideas were exchanged at these "Wistar parties" and the advancement of science was encouraged. After his death the Society continued this practice and the "Wistar Parties" of the Society are held several times each year.[2]

The Society appointed a committee on 3 April 1818 to procure a portrait of Wistar and that year a plaster bust by William Rush was presented by John Vaughan. In 1830 President Du Ponceau wrote Mrs. Mifflin Wistar requesting the loan of a portrait of Wistar by Bass Otis in order that Thomas Sully could make a copy for the Society. Sully completed it in 1830 and it was received from the artist 21 January 1831.[3]

Medical Desk (Fig. 15)

Immediately after his death, Mrs. Wistar presented his medical desk to the Society. The desk remained in Philosophical Hall but its provenance was lost until Secretary I. M. Hays wrote Curator Miller 5 January 1918 that he had "recently discovered that Mrs. Caspar Wistar, a few months after her husband's death, presented his desk here for the use of the Society."[4] Later, on 9 February 1918, Hays wrote Miller again to report that the desk had been repaired and refinished by John Barber. "It took two men over 2 days to do the work."[5]

This is a huge mahogany Philadelphia double-pedestal medical desk made ca. 1780 for Dr. Wistar. The superstructure has a molded rectangular top formed by a pair of hinged ends which open outward 22" each (each contains a lid and a storage space within). These flank a lift-up center section. Opened, a fitted work surface (covered with green baize, and a pigeonhole section with two ivory drawer pulls) is exposed with a fall-front mock drawer, thereby providing much room for work when the good doctor mixed medicines, treated patients, etc. All of this section surmounts a conforming cockbeaded wide drawer with continuous case moldings. The twin pedestals beneath are each fitted with a graduated series of three cockbeaded drawers which are flanked by large brass carrying-handles to the sides, all above a continuous deep-base molding. All the brass is original. The height is 36"; the width (closed) 45¼"; and the depth is 24½".[6]

Fig. 15. Medical Desk

Tambour Desk (Fig. 16)

Over a century and a half after the accession of the medical desk, in 1959, Thomas Wistar, a distant relative, presented a tambour desk with an upper section which had belonged to Caspar Wistar. Its provenance is impeccable, as indicated by a letter from Thomas Wistar: "Dr. Wistar was a brother of my great, great grandfather. The desk was given to my father, Edward Morris Wistar, by the widow of Caspar Wistar's son, Mrs. Mifflin Morris."[7]

This Federal mahogany tambour desk was made in Philadelphia ca. 1795–1800. The tambour door, with turned wooden pulls, slides vertically up the tracked sloping sides, exposing the interior of six small drawers with fruitwood fronts fitted with ivory knob pulls. An inkwell and pen-stand of glass are in the lower right drawer. These small drawers are under seven black-painted pigeonholes. The baize-covered extendable writing surface, which pulls out to 21" deep with three mock drawers behind, is above a cockbeaded wide drawer with turned wooden pulls within three slender case moldings continuing along the sides. These are raised on ringed, slender, tapering, reeded round legs terminating the compressed globous ankles with tall peg feet. Both the tambour cover and the wide drawer have keyholes and there is a key. There is an upper section in the form of a low cabinet of twin double-panel glazed doors enclosing an interior of adjustable shelves. The glass throughout is original. It is 36½" wide; the height is 23¾"; the depth is 9¾". The desk is 41" wide; the height is 35½"; and it is 26" deep.[8]

John Aitken made a tambour desk and book case, much like this but far taller and more elaborate, for George Washington upon his retirement to Mount Vernon.[9]

CASPAR WISTAR

Fig. 16. Tambour Desk and Bookcase

Andirons (Fig. 17)

In 1976 Mrs. Henry Goddard Leach bequeathed to the Society the famous Wistar andirons. They are interesting for their size and unique detail, with etched acorn tops, set upon a slender spool-turned section over festoon-molded square plinths. The plinth steps down into gadrooned apron-molding on cabriole legs with lozenge on the knees and ends in delicately worked hairy paw-feet. They are worked to tops with bold dentate leaf borders joining the plinth base. The wrought-iron supports are surmounted with smaller conforming brass acorns and raised on tapered round legs with square feet. The height is 14″ and the length is 18″.[10]

These are considered the finest of Philadelphia brass andirons and were made ca. 1770. They were executed "with incomparable skill." Such items, with the elaborations and extravagant taste, could be indulged in only by the wealthiest families. They are pictured in *Blue Book, Philadelphia Furniture.*[11]

These andirons have been exhibited many times. The last exhibit was in the Philadelphia Art Museum in the great Bicentennial Exhibition of 1976. The catalogue for that exhibition points out that these were probably made by Daniel King, for the Wistar brass foundry seems to have made nothing but brass buttons, in all sizes. King had cast such hairy paw-feet from carved wooden models for another such pair of andirons.[12]

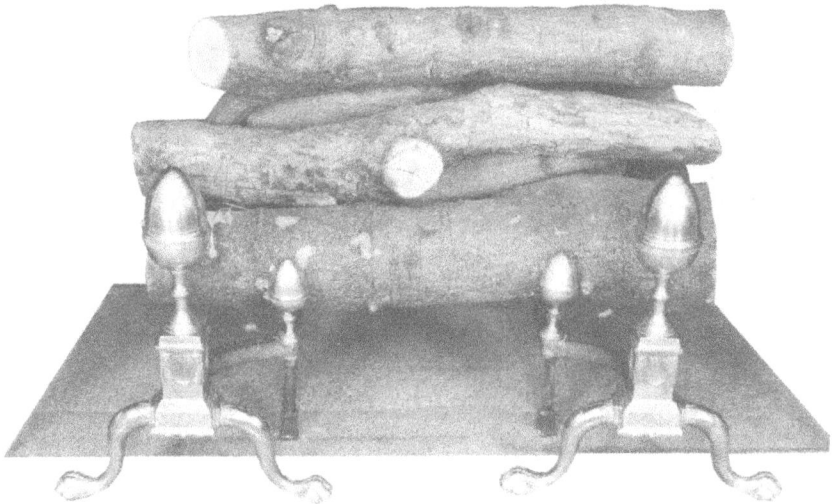

Fig. 17. Andirons

1. C. Wistar "A Description of the Bones Deposited, by the President, in the Museum of the Society, and Represented in the annexed plates," *Trans.*, 4:526ff. George Gaylord Simpson, "The Beginnings of Vertebrate Paleontology in North America," *Proceedings of the American Philosophical Society* (1943), 86:130–88 (hereafter *Proc.*).
2. William Tilghman, *An Eulogium in Commemoration of Doctor Caspar Wistar, late President of the American Philosophical Society Held at Philadelphia for Promoting Useful Knowledge, &c.* (Philadelphia: E. Earle: 1818).
3. Min., 3 April 1818; *Cat. of Portraits*, 104–105.
4. Archives, V, B, 2. I. M. Hays to L. W. Miller; 5 Jan. 1918.
5. Ibid., 9 Feb. 1918.
6. Borodin.
7. Archives. T. Wistar to the APS; 18 Aug. 1959.
8. Borodin.
9. William M. Hornor, *Blue Book, Philadelphia Furniture, William Penn to George Washington* (Highland House: [ca. 1977]), 377 (hereafter *Blue Book*).
10. Borodin.
11. *Blue Book*, plate 106, 97–98.
12. Philadelphia Museum of Art. *Philadelphia. Three Centuries of American Art. Bicentennial Exhibition.* April 11–October 10, 1976. Philadelphia Museum of Art.

Philosophical Society Hall
Philadelphia: 20 April 1798

The Treasurer having been (on Nov.ʳ 7. 1797) authorised to borrow money sufficient to relieve the Mortgage to D.ʳ Franklin. (in 500£)

Resolved. That should the Loan to relieve the Mortgage be made by the Treasurer, that the Presi-dent of the Society be authorised to give his Signature to such new Contract or Mortgage as may be made by the Treasurer in Consequence of the above Resolution & that the Secretary be authorised to place the Seal thereto

Th: Jefferson Presid.ᵗ

JEFFERSON LETTER

Thomas Jefferson
President of the Society 1797–1814

Thomas Jefferson gloried in science and its practical applications. The very title of the Society, The American Philosophical Society held in Philadelphia for Promoting Useful Knowledge, must have held a strong appeal for him. He was elected in 1780 and proved a most valuable member, becoming a councillor, 1781–1786 and 1818–1827; vice-president, 1791–1795; and president, 1797–1814. In addition, he served on many committees, including one which advertised for American antiquities (early colonial history, but especially American Indian artifacts and information) for the Society in 1799.[1] From this committee circular has grown the large collection of American Indian artifacts, now at the University Museum of the University of Pennsylvania, and the massive collection of manuscripts pertaining to American Indians in the library of the Society. Jefferson presented much to the library: the most valuable gift was the original Lewis and Clark journals. His *Notes on Virginia* was another great gift. He wrote this book in reply to a query by the French diplomat in the United States, François de Barbé-Marbois, who wrote to the various states in 1780 concerning the natural history of the United States. This volume, printed in 1782, is Jefferson's reply.

Jefferson was fascinated by the fossil bones found in America and was eager to help the Society amass as much material as possible for its collection of paleontological specimens. He even arranged for William Clark to dig at Big Bone Lick in Kentucky and send the bones to him. These were in large part forwarded to the Society. He and Caspar Wistar published what George Gaylord Simpson states might well be the basis for their being the "fathers of American anatomical paleontology." Jefferson's "Memoir on the discovery of certain bones of a quadruped of the clawed kind in the western part of Virginia" is in the same volume of the *Transactions* as Wistar's "A Description of the Bones Deposited, by the President, in the Museum of the Society."[2]

Jefferson's fame was useful for the Society when he was its president, for many communications were sent to him on scientific subjects and he forwarded many to the Society. His gifts were numerous and his communications to the Society were plentiful. He was very proud of the honor of being elected a member, and later president.

There are several portraits, busts, and representations of Jefferson in the Society. The most perfect is the life study which Thomas Sully made at Monticello in 1821 for the portrait for the United States Military Academy at West Point. There is a Houdon bust of Jefferson in Philosophical Hall which was presented by Elizabeth Rittenhouse Sergeant from the estate of her father, David Rittenhouse, in 1811. Jefferson brought five casts of this bust back from France and, it is believed, presented this one to Rittenhouse.[3]

Polygraph (Fig. 18)

Nicholas P. Trist, a student of Jefferson's, presented a polygraph to the Society on 18 October 1850.[4] It is an elegantly made brass-bound wooden box 8½" by 15" by 3½", with an inlaid top, hinged in three sections to open flat, leaving the central section upright to suspend the two pen-fitted flexible writing arms above the exposed writing surface. An attached brass plate is inscribed: "Hawkins' Patent Polygraph, Manufactured and Sold by I. H. Farthing, No. 43, Cornhill, London, No. 282."[5]

John Isaac Hawkins was an English inventor who lived in Philadelphia about 1800. He was a friend of Charles Willson Peale and invented various devices, such as a "Patent portable grand piano," a formula for waterproofing shoes, and an improvement in distillation. He invented the polygraph about 1802: a device for writing more than one copy of a letter simultaneously, by using pens which are connected by mechanical linkage. Peale crafted polygraphs and sold the first one to Benjamin Henry Latrobe who showed it to Jefferson. Jefferson attempted to arouse interest in the invention, for it produced a perfect facsimile, indistinguishable from the original.[6] Jefferson wrote the comte de Volney, 8 February 1805:

A good invention here, therefore, is such a rarity as it is lawful to offer to the acceptance of a friend. A Mr. Hawkins of Frankford, near Philadelphia, has invented a machine which he calls a polygraph, and which carries, two, three, or four pens. That of two pens, with which I am now writing, is best; and is so perfect that I have laid aside the copying-press, for a twelve-month past, and write always with the polygraph. I have directed one to be made, of which I ask your acceptance.[7]

He wrote James Bowdoin 10 July 1806:

I believe that when you left America the invention of the polygraph had not yet reached Boston. It is for copying with one pen while you write with the other, and without the least additional embarrassment of exertion to the writer. I think it the finest invention of the present age, and so much superior to the copying machine, that the latter will never be continued a day by any one who tries the polygraph. . . . Knowing that you are in the habit of writing much, I have flattered myself that I could add acceptably to your daily convenience by presenting you with one of these delightful machines. I have accordingly had one made, and to be certain of its perfection I have used it myself some weeks, and have the satisfaction to find it the best one I have ever tried; and in the course of two years daily use of them, I have had the opportunity of trying several. As a secretary, which copies for us what we write without the power of revealing it, I find it a most precious possession to a man in public business.[8]

The donor, Nicholas P. Trist, was intimately involved with Jefferson and his family. He studied law with Jefferson, helped Mrs. Martha Jefferson Randolph after Jefferson's death, and married Jefferson's granddaughter. In the Donation Books, date of 18 October 1850, the entry reads: "A Polygraph, or Writing Machine, formerly belonging to, and used by Thomas Jefferson."

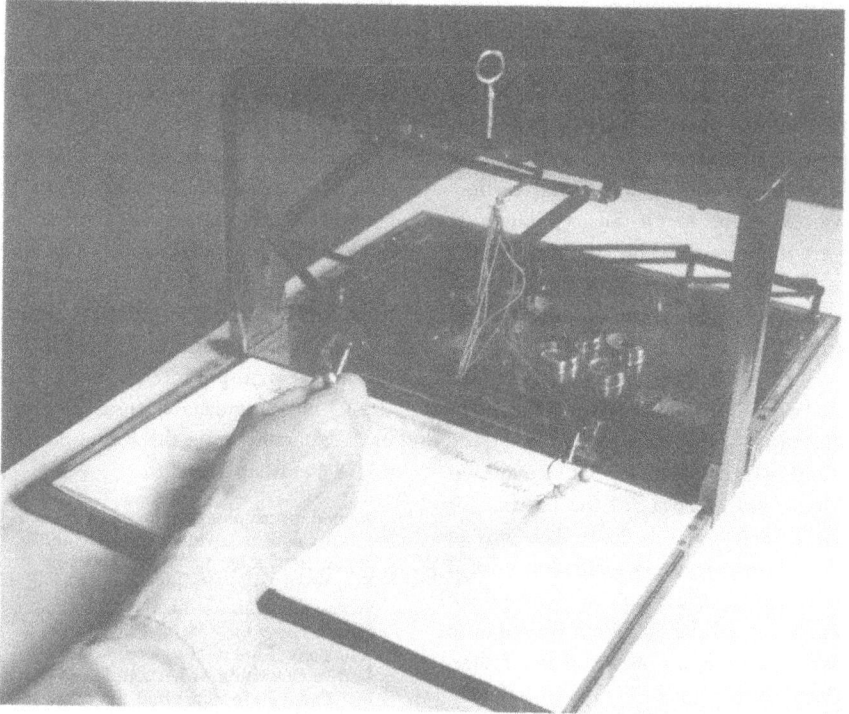

Fig. 18. Polygraph

Windsor Chair (Fig. 19)

This green painted Windsor revolving armchair of Philadelphia manufacture, possibly by Francis Trumbull who made the chairs of the same design for the Carpenters Company Hall in Philadelphia, was purchased by Jefferson in 1776 when he was writing the Declaration of Independence. It is made of an assortment of woods, with mahogany used for the arms. The slender crest rail ends in scrolled ears and is raised on ten plain, round spindles which pass through a semicircular rail. The rail ends in finely knuckled handholds raised on baluster-and-ring turned supports. The supports rest on a slightly peaked circular seat which swivels on a mechanism of four sash pulleys which were probably purchased from Benjamin Randolph. Jefferson had a thin sheet of iron placed on the bottom of the upper section of the chair to keep the poplar wood from being worn too

Fig. 19. Windsor Chair

much by the pulleys. The mechanism rests on a second circular piece of wood which in turn rests on raked bamboo-turned legs joined by ringed bulbous side and medial stretchers. The writing board was added by Jefferson about 1791 and the back of the chair was, at that date, pushed to the edge of the seat so Jefferson could sit down. The legs are replacements which Jefferson installed when he made the chair part of a chaise lounge: the lounge part is still at Monticello. The chair is 43″ high; the seat height is 17¼″; the width is 29″; and the depth is 32½″.[9]

Jefferson probably told Randolph how to alter the chair and thereby created a revolving chair. Revolving chairs were scarce in America and Jefferson was castigated by the Federalists for boasting of a chair "which had the miraculous quality of allowing a person seated in it to turn his head without moving his tail."[10]

Mrs. Martha Jefferson Randolph, Jefferson's daughter, gave this chair to Judge John Kintzing Kane, a secretary of the Society and later its president, and he presented it to the Society 20 April 1838:

> I beg leave to entrust to the care of the Society the writing chair used by Mr. Jefferson at Philadelphia, while preparing the Declaration of Independence. At the close of the congressional labours of 1776, he carried it with him to Virginia; and after his death, it was carefully preserved by his family with a few other personal memorials. His daughter, the late Mrs. Randolph, did me the honour to present it to me some eighteen months ago, and it is through her that I became acquainted with its history.

> It is a plain, old fashioned Windsor armchair, with a circular back; a writing leaf or table is fixed upon the right arm, and the body of the chair revolves about a pivot. It has been repaired since it came into my possession, but without changing its form in any respect.[11]

In 1966 Ada G. Straus, an antique dealer in Baltimore, Maryland, presented four small pieces which had been broken from this chair. When the chair was restored in 1975 and the legs replaced by legs typical of a Windsor chair of the late eighteenth century, these pieces were replaced on the chair in their correct position.[12]

1. *Trans.* 5:ix–xi.
2. Ibid., 4:246–60 (Jefferson), 526–31 (Wistar).
3. *Cat. of Portraits*, 52–55.
4. Min., 18 Oct. 1850.
5. Borodin.
6. *Cat. of Insts.*, 60.
7. T. Jefferson to comte de Volney, 8 Feb. 1805. Albert Ellery Bergh, ed., *The Writings of Thomas Jefferson* (Washington, 1907) 11:62–69.
8. T. Jefferson to J. Bowdoin, 10 July 1806. Ibid., 118–21.
9. Borodin.
10. See for a detailed study: Charles L. Grandquist, "Thomas Jefferson's "whirligig chairs," *Antiques* 109: no. 5.
11. Archives. J. K. Kane to APS; 20 April 1838.
12. Richardson.

John Vaughan
Secretary, Treasurer and Librarian
1784–1841

John Vaughan was the son of Samuel Vaughan, APS 1784, who oversaw the building of Philosophical Hall and was named benefactor to the Society for his generous gift of scientific instruments. Perhaps his greatest gift, however, was his son, John, who was trained by Joseph Priestley. John became a merchant with an intense interest in science and, as a bachelor, lived in Philosophical Hall for many years.

He was active in the Unitarian movement and was instrumental in the erection of a church in Philadelphia for the group. He was outstanding socially and attended many public and private functions. His interest in science was well known and he served on many committees of the Society. He was a great donor to the library, presenting volume after volume throughout his long life. He left many books to the library in his will, as well as three articles of furniture which he knew, from intimate experience, would be of use.

Vaughan had been so active and such a major figure in the Society that it was resolved at a meeting of 20 June 1823 to have his portrait painted, ". . . on consideration of his extraordinary care and attention to the library, for his great exertions in procuring contributions for it and for his own, very liberal donations. . . . [The portrait was to be] preserved in their Hall, as a token of the sense which they entertain of his merits and services."[1]

Thomas Sully painted this portrait which hangs today in the librarian's office. Vaughan's heir presented a bust of Vaughan 21 October 1842, which is in the reading room of the library.[2]

JOHN VAUGHAN

Mahogany Marble Top Table (Fig. 20)

This American late-Federal mahogany marble-top table of the late first quarter of the nineteenth century was probably made for Vaughan. It has an overhanging rectangular top of green Connecticut marble above a shaped apron with square corners and is raised on bold ring-turned vasiform legs conjoined by a deep stretcher shelf and ending in peg-feet. It is 28″ high, 36″ wide and 23½″ deep. It was probably made to hold scientific instruments and it now bears the astronomical transit telescope made by David Rittenhouse (see above, p. 23).[3]

Fig. 20. Mahogany Marble Top Table

Mahogany Sideboard (Fig. 21)

This Federal mahogany Philadelphia early nineteenth-century sideboard has a overhanging rectangular top surmounted on the sides and back by a shallow domical-shaped splashboard. The front consists of a single deep drawer above a deep scooped apron flanked by twin banks of six graduated drawers, all of which have cockbeaded edges and ringed round brass pulls. There are short ringed slender legs of compressed ovoid section on button feet. The height is 35½"; the width is 72½"; and the depth is 24½".[4]

It was given very hard usage over the years and was relegated to the attic of Philosophical Hall for some time. It was restored and refinished in 1960.

Hanging above this sideboard today is the original 1701 Charter of Privileges which William Penn granted the colony of Pennsylvania. It is flanked by two Houdon plaster busts of former members of the Society: Ann Robert Jacques Turgot, who coined the famous epigram for Franklin, *Eripuit coelo fulmen, septruque tyrannis*; and Thomas Jefferson (see above, p. 36).

Fig. 21. Mahogany Sideboard

Mahogany Drop-Leaf Pembroke Table (Fig. 22)

This large Federal mahogany drop-leaf Pembroke table was probably made in Philadelphia in the early nineteenth century. It has a single-plank rectangular overhanging top hinged with rounded shallow drop-leaves which can be raised on hinged swing supports, flanking a frieze drawer with a turned wooden pull above a cockbeaded edge molding. The table is raised on tapered reeded round legs which terminate in compressed globous ankles with deep peg-feet and turned at top with deep collars. The height is 28¾"; the length is 42"; the width (closed) is 25"; and the width (opened) is approximately 50".[5]

This table was used wherever needed and was scratched and battered. It was restored and refinished in 1960.

Fig. 22. Mahogany Drop-Leaf Pembroke Table

Windsor Chair (Fig. 23)

Vaughan left a bequest of miscellaneous articles of furniture to William Warren, the building superintendent of Philosophical Hall. The Society purchased several articles of this furniture, including two armchairs of the Windsor type, from Warren later in 1841.[6] There is one such chair in the Society which is commonly called the

John Vaughan chair and probably is the one Windsor chair remaining from this purchase.

It is a Federal Philadelphia yellow-painted multiwood Windsor armchair made ca. 1810–1820. It has a straight crest rail raised on seven slender bamboo-turned spindles which are flanked by conforming bold stiles, fitted with conforming arms and supports. They all terminate in a grooved and scooped saddle-shaped seat which is raised on raked bamboo-turned legs and stretchers. The underside of the seat is incised with the inscription: "Mary's seat / Sept. 4 1865." The height is 34¼"; the width is 18½"; and the depth is 16".[7]

1. Min., 20 June 1823.
2. Cat. of Portraits, 94–96.
3. Borodin.
4. Ibid.
5. Ibid.
6. Treas. Recs., 1841.
7. Borodin.

Fig. 23. Windsor Chair

Joseph Bonaparte
American Philosophical Society
1823

Bonaparte Chair (Fig. 24)

Joseph Bonaparte, comte de Survilliers, at one time king of Naples and then of Spain, was the eldest son of a talented and brilliant family. He was also the mildest of the Bonapartes. He had a particularly intimate connection with the emperor and tried to check the excesses of his younger brother. He was just, tenacious, considerate and forbearing and was an infallible regent for France when the emperor was away,

> proof against all assaults, temptations, and seductions. . . . His predilections for peace were manifested [in his work for the peace of Amiens] and in battle he displayed the intrepid composure of a valiant general. During the four years of his reign on a bed of roses in Naples, and the five under a crown of thorns in Spain, he was and judged a philosopher on a throne.

After the battle of Waterloo, he and his famous brother chartered ships to escape. The former emperor was captured, but Joseph was more fortunate and landed in New York. He moved to

Fig. 24. Bonaparte Chair

Philadelphia and lived in various houses until the state of New Jersey passed an act which permitted him to own property in that state. He purchased about 1,800 acres near Bordentown and built a great house, Point Breeze, which promptly burned. He built another on the same site in which he lived. This was perhaps the most elaborate and sumptuously furnished home in the United States.

Joseph was greatly respected in the United States as a truly amiable man, pleasant to all, without pride and he was generous.[1] He was immensely wealthy and gave away many paintings, jewels, articles of furniture, etc. A record was kept of his gifts and an entry reads that in 1836 he presented to the Society: "1 coupe antique et l'ouvrage de P[rin]ce Charles sur les animaux d'[Italie]."[2] The Donation Book of the Society records that Joseph Bonaparte "presented the antique vase, a kylix, and three volumes by Charles Lucien Bonaparte, prince de Canino: *Iconografia della fauna Italica per le quattro classi degli animali vertebrati.*" Roma: 1832–41.[3]

The ancient capital of Etruria, Vitulonia, once stood on part of the prince's estate. The kylix is a Greek Attic red-figured kylix with alien stem and foot, ca. 470–450 B.C. It is now in the University Museum, University of Pennsylvania. The publication is still in the library.[4]

The comte de Survilliers gave much furniture to his friends when he left the United States, and one of his particular friends was Nathaniel Chapman, of the Society. A chair from this gift was delivered by J. McClure Hamilton on 11

March 1886. His father, George Hamilton, had directed that the chair be presented to the Society where Joseph had been a member. He wrote that it was "a red rep. Arm Chair" which had been given by Jerome to Chapman. George Hamilton purchased it from Mrs. Chapman.[5]

This Empire mahogany upholstered reclining chair was probably made in either Philadelphia or New York, ca. 1820–1830. It is of Roman curule form and has a rounded X-form profile of opposing scrolls which flair backward slightly along the tall back. The upholstered arms roll downward into comma-shaped open scrolls which contrast with the scroll of the seat. The legs are of square section and end in casters. The height is 39"; the width is 24"; and the depth is 34".[6]

This chair has been a favorite of many of the members and has received constant wear. It has been recovered many times and was repaired and recovered last in 1976.

1. Charles J. Ingersoll, "Obituary of J. Bonaparte," *Proc.*, 6:71–76.
2. "Memorandum—objets donnés ou vendus." Mailliard Family Collection at Yale University Library, Notebook, 1843–1841, relating to the property of Joseph Bonaparte (copy at The Athenaeum of Philadelphia).
3. APS Donation Book, 1836.
4. William B. Dinsmoor, "Early American Studies of Mediterranean Archaeology," *Proc.*, 87:90–91, fig. 13; Mary Hamilton Swindler, "Another Vase by the Master of the Penthesilea Cylix," *American Journal of Archaeology* (1909), 13:142–50, figs. 1–7.
5. Archives. J. M. Hamilton to APS, 11 March 1886.
6. Borodin.

Robert Eglesfeld Griffith, Jr.
Curator of the Society
1829, 1831–1836

Griffith was born in Philadelphia and in 1820 he took his M.D. degree from the University of Pennsylvania with a thesis on the "Stomach and its Functions." He practiced medicine in Philadelphia and was physician to the Board of Health. He became professor of materia medica at the Philadelphia College of Pharmacy in 1835 but left the next year to become professor of materia medica, therapeutics, hygiene and medical jurisprudence at the University of Maryland. In 1838 he was appointed professor of practice, obstetrics and medical jurisprudence at the University of Virginia. He later returned to Philadelphia and was active in the Franklin Institute and the Academy of Natural Sciences in Philadelphia, becoming vice-president of the Academy.

Dr. Griffith was made a member of the Society in 1828 and served several years as curator. He published, edited, and translated several important volumes on therapeutic medicine, pharmacopoeias, materia medica, medical botany, and medical jurisprudence. He became an outstanding botanist and conchologist and presented his conchological collection to the Academy of Natural Sciences of Philadelphia. He began a large work on conchology and planned a book on "The Botany in the Bible." Asa Gray and other outstanding botanists urged him to complete this last work.[1]

Mrs. Roland R. Foulke bequeathed to the Society in 1955 several pieces of furniture which once belonged to her ancestor, Dr. Griffith. She in-

sisted, however, that a written acknowledgment must be sent to her that the Society would never part with them.

President Owen J. Roberts wrote her 25 May 1954 that her insistence on such a promise was unnecessary.

> The Council of the American Philosophical Society which alone is competent to act in this matter will not meet again until late in the autumn. I suggest, however, that you can obtain your objective with perfect satisfaction by providing in your Will that these articles are to go to The American Philosophical Society held at Philadelphia for Promoting Useful Knowledge on condition that the Society in accepting them agrees to retain them as its own property and not to part with them.

She replied 31 May 1954 that, since these items were to be a memorial to her grandfather, she must insist. Her "experience in the past in leaving our possessions to an institution and the institution selling or exchanging them . . . would grieve me greatly." She could not "leave them to any Society unless I have such an assurance." After all, she wrote later, these articles were brought from "England at about 1778 & were in Robert E. Griffith's house in the Park on the Schuylkill River."

The Council of the Society bowed to her request on 11 November 1954. President Roberts wrote 23 November that

> The Officers and Councillors were greatly pleased to learn of your proposed gift in memory of your ancestor and unanimously accepted the gift. The Council resolved that this action should form a part of the Minutes of the Council Meeting and that the gift should be maintained as an asset of the Society and should not be sold or otherwise disposed of. . . . The gift and the conditions accepted by the Council were announced to the full membership of the Society at its meeting on November 12 and met with unanimous approval.[2]

"Argand" Oil Lamp (Fig. 25)

This "old whale oil candelabrum" is an English early Victorian bronze "Argand" oil lamp which was made ca. 1840. It has a bell-shaped well-cover surmounted with a pineapple finial above the outward flaring handles of swirled anthemian shape. A rim of stiff pointed leaves suspended with fleurette-cut button-and-spear prism drops is above a pair of slender arms which support vented cylindrical burners with frosted glass pyriform shades. The ringed urn-form standard is on a stepped square base with button feet. Some of the prisms are replacements, possibly of the third quarter of the nineteenth century. It is 20" high and 17" wide. At one time the lamp was altered to burn gas and the pipe remains on the bottom.[3]

This lamp rests today on the "Foulke" sideboard (see p. 53), above which hangs the only known portrait of Benjamin Franklin's wife, Deborah Read Franklin. The portrait is attributed to Benjamin Wilson after an American portrait.

Fig. 25. "Argand" Oil Lamp

Fig. 26. Bronze Candelabra

Pair of Bronze Candelabra
(Fig. 26)

A pair of English bronze candelabra which were made ca. 1835 rest on the mantels which flank the John Vaughan sideboard (see page 43). Each candelabrum has an arrangement of three-petaled sockets and bobeches which are suspended with cushion-and-spear colorless prism drops: the center cluster is plain and the side clusters are cut with fleurettes. They are raised on a leafy standard upon a leaf-molded stepped rectangular base on gadrooned button feet. The outer prism drops may be replacements of the third quarter of the nineteenth century. Their height is 11½"; their width is 10"; and their depth is 4".[4]

Mahogany Drop-Leaf Table
(Fig. 27)

This Federal inlaid mahogany drop-leaf Pembroke table was made in Philadelphia around 1790–1800. The overhanging top is hinged with rounded drop-leaves forming an oval, and raised on hinged swing-supports flanking a slightly rounded frieze drawer with cockbeaded border. There is a string-inlaid reserve border and oval brass bail handle above a banded edge raised on stringed tapering, square legs with banded, crossband cuffs. The height is 28½"; the length is 32"; the width (closed) is 19½"; and the width (opened) is approximately 46".[5]

Fig. 27. Mahogany Drop-Leaf Table

Mahogany Foulke Sideboard (Fig. 28)

This American Empire marble-top mahogany sideboard was made in Phila-delphia ca. 1835. The slightly over-hanging marble top is above a protruding frieze fitted with a handleless drawer in book-matched veneer of boldly figured crotch mahogany beneath a molded top edge continued along the sides of the case. These are all raised on freestanding pilasters in the form of Ionic columns above a conforming veneered platform on massive paw-feet at the front (and round legs behind). The columns stand before the recessed back which is hinged with a pair of mirrored doors; the doors were possibly added at a later date, converting what was probably a pier table to a sideboard. The height is 39½"; the width is 42"; and, the depth is 18".[6]

Fig. 28. *Mahogany Foulke Sideboard*

Brass Andirons (Fig. 29)

One of a pair of American brass andirons which were made (possibly in Philadelphia or Boston?) ca. 1840. Each has a ringed and paneled ovoid knob raised on an elaborately shaped standard on paneled and ringed sections which rest upon a pair of Baroque-style scroll legs of compressed bombé outline which are raised on four small bulbous feet. The wrought-iron rail is raised on a round rear leg and surmounted with a conforming brass knob. The height of the andirons is 20″; their length is 21½″. There is also a matching set of fire tools, tongs and shovel, with a stand and a fire fender.[7]

This pair of andirons and the fire tools and fender are kept in a fireplace in Philosophical Hall.

Fig. 29. Brass Andirons

*Mahogany Drop-leaf Pedestal
Table (Fig. 30)*

This is a Philadelphia classical
mahogany drop-leaf pedestal table which
was made ca. 1820–1830. It has a rectangular overhanging top, hinged with
boldly scalloped shallow drop-leaves
which are raised on hinged swing-supports flanking a cockbeaded frieze
drawer with brass pull at each end above
cockbeaded edge moldings and protruding corners suspended with stepped ring
drops. These rest on an urn-form pedestal raised on molded sabre legs ending in
brass paw-feet. The height is 28½"; the
length is 40"; the width when closed is
23"; and the width when open approximately 52".[8]

A table like this was made by
Ephraim Haines.[9]

1. Howard A. Kelly and Walter L. Burrage. *Dictionary of American Medical Biographies* (Boston, 1971).
2. None of the pieces received from Mrs. Foulke is of the eighteenth century. She must have repeated stories she heard about the furniture as a child, saying that they came from England at about 1778. APS. Archives. Owen J. Roberts to Mrs. R. R. Foulke, 25 May 1954; Mrs. R. R. Foulke to Owen J. Roberts, 31 May 1954; Ibid., n.d.; Owen J. Roberts to Mrs. R. R. Foulke, 23 Nov., 1954.
3. Borodin.
4. Ibid.
5. Ibid.
6. Ibid.
7. Ibid.
8. Ibid.
9. Philadelphia Museum of Art. Original photographs of an exhibit of Henry Connelly and Ephraim Haines.

Fig. 30. *Mahogany Drop-Leaf Pedestal Table*

George Bacon Wood
President of the Society
1859–1879 Bookcase

Wood was a physician who received the M.D. degree from the University of Pennsylvania in 1818. He was made professor of chemistry at the Philadelphia College of Pharmacy and held the post until he was given the chair of materia medica there. In 1835 he took the chair of materia medica at the University of Pennsylvania which he held until 1850 when he was transferred to the chair of the theory and practice of medicine, his last appointment.

He took a prominent part in the editorship of the *North American Medical and Surgical Journal*. With others, he revised the *Pharmacopeia of the United States* and it became the standard authority in 1830 for the preparation of official medicines throughout the country. Later, the same group compiled a very elaborate commentary on the *Pharmacopeia*, published as the *Dispensatory of the United States*. Around 120,000 copies were sold during his lifetime.

Fig. 31. Mahogany and Brass Bookcase

In 1835 Wood was appointed one of the attending physicians to the Pennsylvania Hospital and he practiced there faithfully until 1859. He loved his work and was indefatigable at it. Open-handed benevolence was one of his prominent traits. It was said that "No man has ever done so much as he, to form and influence medical opinion in America upon both practical and ethical questions. His teaching was dictated by good judgment, careful study, and, above all, the highest principles of rectitude and honor."

Dr. Wood became a member of the Society in 1829 and was active in its functions. He traveled widely and visited Europe three times. While in Europe he attended to the Society's business in Russia and in France.[1] In Italy, while visiting, he ordered Domenico Menconi to carve a life-size marble bust of Franklin after the huge plaster bust, attributed to Houdon, owned by an English banker, Mr. Packinham. He presented this bust to the Society on 2 January 1863.[2] He published several articles in the *Proceedings* regarding the fertilizing and renewing action of the alkali potassia on the growth of fruit trees, potatoes, wheat, etc.[3] He was elected president in 1859 and continued his active interest in the Society. A portrait by Margaret Lesley Bush-Brown, after the portrait by Samuel B. Waugh at the University of Pennsylvania, was ordered by the Society and exhibited 21 July 1882.[4]

His marriage was childless but the memory of Wood and his interest in the Society remained among his relatives. As late as 1935 Walter Wood left a bequest to the Society in memory of his kinsman: a marble bust of George Bacon Wood.[5] Included in this bequest was a bookcase which had belonged to Dr. Wood.[6]

This large American mahogany and glass bookcase (Fig. 31) is probably of Philadelphia manufacture of the second half of the nineteenth century. The original base is lacking. The upper section has a plain cornice molding above a set of four eight-panel glazed doors with Gothic arch top panels, enclosing wooden shelves above a shallow bracket foot of later date. The bookcase is 72" high; it is 97" wide; and it is 13" deep.[7]

1. Henry Hartshorne, "Memoir of G. B. Wood, M.D., LL.D.," *Proc.* 19:118–52.
2. *Cat. of Portraits*, 35.
3. *Proc.* 11 and 12.
4. Min., 21 July 1882.
5. *Cat. of Portraits*, 107.
6. *Proc*, 75:xii, xxvi (for Walter Wood bequest).
7. Borodin.

ISAAC MINIS HAYS

Isaac Minis Hays
Secretary and Librarian
1897–1922

Hays's life had two foci: Benjamin Franklin and the Society. A physician, he did not practice, but joined the staff of the *American Journal* and was an active member of the American Medical Association. He gained renown as an editor. He was interested in the better cataloguing of the surgeon general's library and worked on the College of Physicians of Philadelphia library committee. He saw the recataloguing of that library and helped rewrite the rules for the better functioning of the library.

He became a member of the Society in 1886 and in 1897 was a secretary and became acting librarian. As acting librarian, Hays began to suggest measures of reform for the Society and his duties grew until he was, in effect, the first executive officer. He handled the correspondence and "personally edited and supervised the printing of 27 volumes of *Proceedings* and *Transactions*." He seems to have dominated practically all of the committees and carried forward the Society's work.

During his tenure the library was catalogued and working rules were written. In order to help make the library better known, he prepared calendars to the General George Weedon, the Richard Henry Lee and the Nathanael Greene papers. He worked manfully in arranging and preparing for the hugely successful bicentennial of Benjamin Franklin's birth and oversaw both the calendaring and publication of the calendars of the massive collection of Franklin's manuscripts in the Library.

At this time interest in the Society was reawakened and plans were soon made to build another building and abandon Philosophical Hall. The library was bursting at the seams and the members did not have enough rooms for meetings. Hays determined to leave his residual estate to the Society to help furnish the rooms in the proposed building to endow it for future use. He was an active member of the Wistar Party and the Wistar Association presented his portrait by Lazar Radniz to the Society in 1917, thereby marking the anniversary of his twenty-five years of service.[1]

In 1974 the residuary estate was settled and, in keeping with the terms of the will, most of the furnishings were sold. The Society had been unable to move from Philosophical Hall and build a new building so the furnishings were not needed for the purpose that Hays had planned. A few items of the furniture were retained by the Society.

Bookcases (Fig. 32)

In 1937 the Hays house was sold and from that house came five Victorian bookcases. They are of walnut and glass, made by Philadelphia workmen during the last quarter of the nineteenth century. Each has a recessed upper section of two or three pairs of glazed and cockbeaded cabinet doors which enclose walnut shelves beneath a plain cyma-recta cornice. Below is a base hinged with a conforming arrangement of short-door inset panels of incised double borders within conforming cockbead bezels. All have been reconstructed and restored and the moldings and glazed doors are of later date.[2]

Fig. 32. Bookcases

Drop-Leaf Table (Fig. 33)

This Federal inlaid mahogany drop-leaf Pembroke table was made in Philadelphia ca. 1790. The hinged oval drop-leaf top is above a drawered bow front and conforming mock-drawer reverse, flanked by lightwood inlaid corners simulating fluting. The square tapered legs have stringed borders and cross-band cuffs. The height is 28½"; the length is 32"; the closed width is 21½"; and the open width is 40¼".[3] This table is depicted in *Blue Book, Philadelphia Furniture*.[4]

Fig. 33. Drop-Leaf Table

Fig. 34. Hepplewhite Style Settee

Hepplewhite Style Settee (Fig. 34)

This Federal inlaid mahogany Hepplewhite-style upholstered settee was made in Philadelphia, probably by William Rigby for it bears the initials WR. It has a straight crest rail centered with a shallow, flat arch and flanked by sloping sides. The sides terminate in short mahogany handholds which are raised on freestanding inverted vasiform supports on flared and tapered legs. The settee is inlaid with lightwood stringing. It has been restored and reupholstered in pink leaf-figured damask. It is 62½" long, 35" high at the back, and 26½" deep.[5] This settee is depicted in *Blue Book, Philadelphia Furniture*.[6]

Regency Side Chairs (Fig. 35)

This set of four Philadelphia Regency classical mahogany side chairs was made ca. 1810–1820. Each chair has a curved and backward-scrolled crest rail inlaid with a plain reserve of highly figured mahogany veneer and raised above a slender slat of opposed S-scrolls, terminating in rosettes and leafage upon a reeded crossbar. The tapered rounded stiles continue along the upholstered slip-seat and slender rail and are raised on plain sabre legs. The seats have been reupholstered. The height of the chairs is 31″; their seat-height is 18″; their depth is 20½″; and their width is 18″.[7]

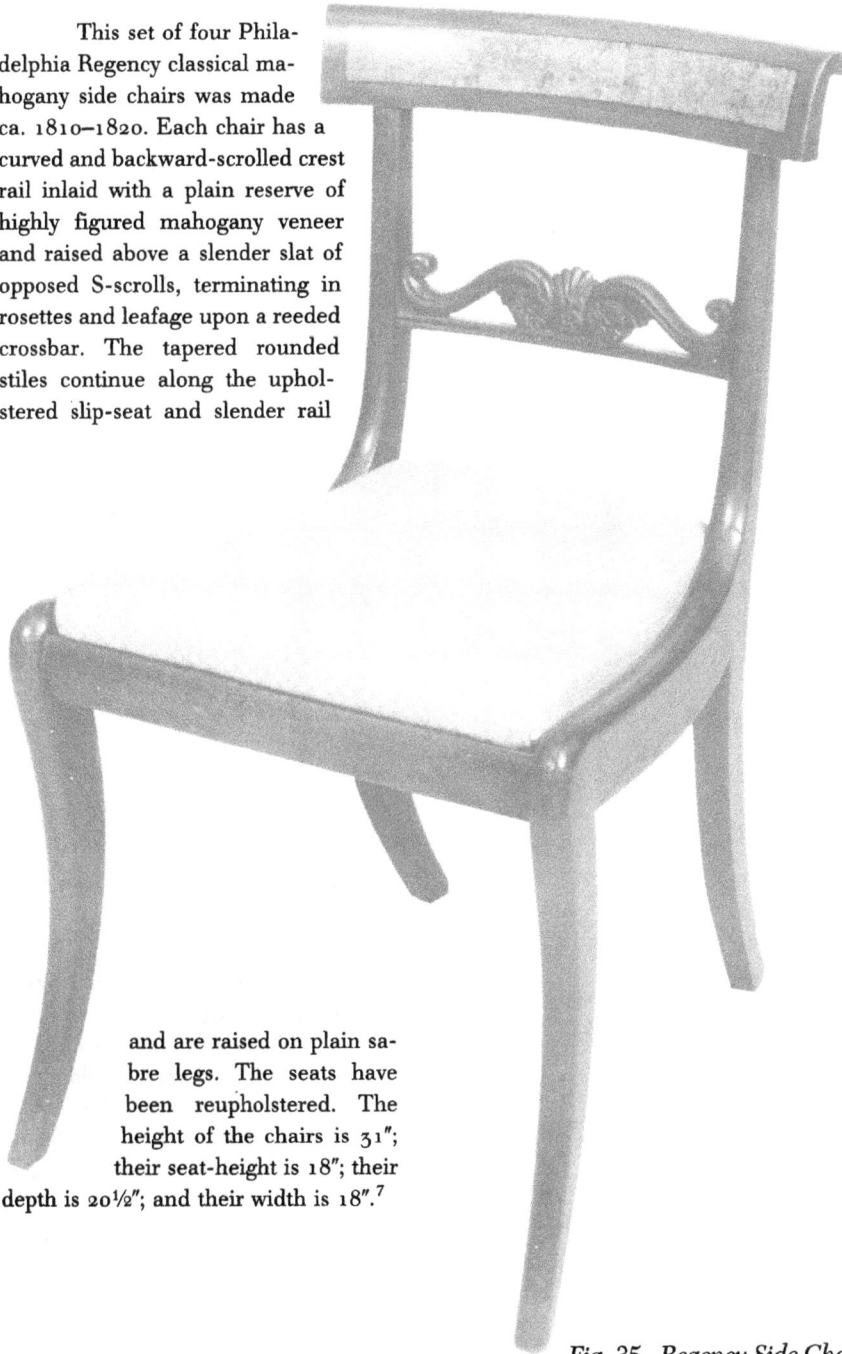

Fig. 35. Regency Side Chair

Folding Top Gate-Leg Card Tables (Fig. 36)

This pair of inlaid mahogany folding top gate-leg card tables are possibly of Philadelphia manufacture, ca. 1795. Each has a rectangular folding top with inset ovolo corners, inlaid with double-stringed edges and a broad band border above a conformingly shaped apron inlaid with plain string reserves and slender banded edge raised on stringed tapering square legs with crossband cuffs. Their height is 29″; their length is 35½″; their width (closed) is 17½″; and their width (opened) is 35″.[8]

Fig. 36b. Folding Top Gate-Leg Card Tables

1. Whitfield J. Bell, Jr., "I. Minis Hays, Secretary, Librarian, and Benefactor of the American Philosophical Society," *Proc.* 119:401–11.
2. Borodin.
3. Ibid.
4. *Blue Book*, plate 395.
5. Borodin.
6. *Blue Book*, plate 412.
7. Borodin.
8. Ibid.

Henry Allen Moe
President of the Society 1959–1970

Secretary-Bookcase (Fig. 37)

Henry Allen Moe was wounded in an accident in World War I and both legs were fractured. They never healed and throughout his life he suffered from an intractable and painful bone infection. While in the hospital he applied for a Rhodes scholarship and received it. He attended Brasenose College where he took the B.A. degree in jurisprudence and, after studying law at the Inns of Court, London, he was admitted to the bar of England as a barrister of the Inner Temple.

When he returned to the United States to begin the practice of law he was recommended to Senator Simon Guggenheim and was asked to draw up plans for a foundation to be established in memory of his son, John Simon Guggenheim. After lengthy consultations with educators throughout the United States, Moe presented his plan and the senator was so pleased with it that Moe was named its secretary and administrator in 1925.

It opened a great career for Moe and he made the Foundation what it is— one of the world's noblest

Fig. 37. Secretary-Bookcase

and most productive benefactors of scholarship, science and the fine arts.

He brought to the post a rare combination of personal charm, and a talent for friendship, a wide range of intellectual interests, energy and enthusiasm, a tenacious memory, organizational ability, a lawyer's decisiveness without legalistic pedantry, critical judgment tempered by generosity. The foundation became judge of a high court of humanities, science, and the fine arts.[1]

Moe inaugurated something new to the academic world: the award of Guggenheim Fellowships to novelists, poets, painters, etc., rather than to scholars and scientists. Honors flowed upon him from Brasenose College, Oxford University, the Museum of Modern Art, the Marine Biological Laboratories at Woods Hole, Massachusetts, and the like. He was made first chairman of the newly founded National Endowment for the Humanities in 1966.

He was proud of being president of the Society, "occupying Franklin's chair." He served on many committees and was diligent in fulfilling the duties of all posts. He enjoyed his membership and attended meetings regularly. A portrait was commissioned from Philadelphia artist Franklin Watkins in 1970. It "reflects Henry Moe's strength and courage, his wisdom and his devotion to scholarship, his breadth of interests, his sense of responsibility and his liberality."[2]

Mrs. Edith Moe presented in 1977 in honor of her husband a beautiful English secretary bookcase which Moe had used in his office over the years and which he greatly admired.[3] She also edited, and the Society published, a collection of some of Moe's articles: *The Power of Freedom in Human Affairs.*

This English mahogany secretary bookcase was made ca. 1770–1780. It is in two sections: the upper section has a delicately carved and pierced swan's neck pediment with a central-urn finial suspended with swags adjoining the leafy rosette terminals above a central shell-carved plinth. These are over a key-fret frieze molding and a pair of glazed doors of interlaced heart-and-diamond mullion work which encloses the interior of wooden shelves. The lower section has a straight front of four cockbeaded drawers with brass pulls flanked by chamfered corners of blind-fret carving over bracket-chamfered feet. The uppermost drawer simulates an arrangement of three drawers and is hinged to fall outward into a writing board. The interior of the desk houses a row of four small square drawers at each end; the center has a long drawer over three open shelves, flanked by a closed compartment with a plain door. Paper pockets with simulated book ends are at each side of these enclosures (a simple and unique arrangement). The height of the top is 53⅝"; the height of the bottom is 44". The overall width is 43¾" and the depth is 22½".[4]

1. George Washington Corner, "Henry Allen Moe," *Yearbook* (1977), 103–109.
2. Ibid.
3. *Yearbook* (1977), 128.
4. Borodin.

Ballot Boxes (Fig. 38)

Inventions were important to the Society, not only for the advancement of "useful knowledge," but also because the Society offered upon occasion the Magellanic Premium for the most useful invention in certain fields. This is the earliest premium awarded by a learned society in the United States and it continues to be awarded. Some of the inventions forwarded to the Society had three-dimensional models and many of these remain in the possession of the Society. I. B. Cohen, as curator of the Society, wrote L. P. Eisenhart, executive officer of the Society, on 21 February 1958 that these mechanical models of the late eighteenth and early nineteenth centuries were worthy of a catalogue and that such models "are so rare that they have all an intrinsic interest."[1]

Among these models are four ballot boxes, all of which have been used. Colonial Pennsylvanians considered themselves Englishmen and they followed English customs in voting for elections, either by voice vote or the raising of hands. Elections for officers and membership in the Society, perforce, followed the English custom and there is no mention of "secret" balloting—nor for the need of it—in the Minutes. Then, at the beginning of the nineteenth century, English reformers agitated for the use of a ballot box (to be used behind screens) to insure secret elections. The idea caught on at once in the United States and the Society received these boxes as gifts from members. They range from a simple to an elegant and beautiful design. Insofar as can be determined, these four are the total number of boxes presented.[2]

Edward H. Pinto, in *Treen and Other Wooden Bygones*, states that in the beginning there were at least two types of boxes: those which

> had single compartments into which hands were thrust through a circular [opening]. ... The balls fell into a drawer below the opening; when the drawer was opened, if it contained all white balls, the candidate was elected; if there were one or more black balls in the drawer, he was "black-balled."

> In the other method of balloting, the balls need only be of one colour, because the box itself is divided into two compartments, for the "Ayes" and "Noes" respectively. The single entry box is still used, but when the hand is inserted in the circular opening, it is found that inside there is a division, and the ball can be dropped to the left or right, into either of two drawers.[3]

The Society possesses two examples of the first and one of the second, as well as a round ballot box with twelve drawers.

The two specimens of the first type were presented by the Bostonian, Benjamin Dearborn. This prolific inventor created a spring scale, grist mill, candlestick and a "faculty for casting interest." He published a description of the latter in 1805 and donated a copy of the invention to the Society. He was elected a member in 1808 and presented his first ballot box in that year. On it, in Secretary John Vaughan's hand, is written: "Inventor. Presented by Benjamin Dearborn: Feb. 5, 1808." It is an oblong, rectangular case raised on short ringed vasiform legs with cuffed feet beneath plain-turned colonette corners. The legs are surmounted with simple button-caps. The top of the box is a shallow tray. There is a narrow compartment at the left with a lift-lid. This lid opens to a larger area, part of which is also accessible by a short drawer. Above the drawer is a hole through which tallies

Fig. 38a. Ballot Boxes

could be dropped. There is a carrying handle on the underside. The ballot box is 12" high, 10" wide and 7" deep.[4]

Dearborn wrote on 11 April 1823 and presented an "improved" ballot box "calculated to conceal the manner of Voting and to be used by the Society at their elections."[5] This is identical to the one presented in 1808, but more elegant. The legs are more elaborate and the plain-turned colonette corners are surmounted with urn-turned finials. It is 13½" high, 10" wide, and it is 10½" deep.[6]

The second type of ballot box was presented by Jonathan Williams, a nephew of Benjamin Franklin. A merchant, he was active in the French trade during the American Revolution and he returned to the United States with Franklin when they made their thermometric observations on the Gulf Stream. He was made a member of the Society in 1787 and was active in it, making several gifts, including a patent on the better claying of sugar.

Around 1810 Williams presented the ballot box which the Society accepted as an "invention" and used. Nothing was said of this gift until 4 March 1814 when the members ordered that thanks be given him for the "very useful & ingenious balloting-box" which he had contributed "some considerable time since, but the acknowledgment of which appears to have been hitherto omitted."[7] It is a birdhouse-shaped wooden box with straight sides beneath a peaked roof of two planks, stenciled "Reject" on the left side and "Admit" on the right. A circular hole is in the front through which tallies could be dropped in separate drawers to the right and left. The base drawers are incised along the

edges to simulate cockbeading. It is 9" high, 10" wide and 10½" deep.[8]

Thomas U. Walter, who became a member in 1839, presented another type of balloting box in 1840. A native Philadelphian, he studied with William Strickland and, as an architect, built Moyamensing Prison in Philadelphia. The most ambitious work of the classical period of American architecture, Founders Hall of Girard College, Philadelphia, was designed by him in 1833 and was completed in 1847. He became architect for the Capitol in Washington in 1851 and retained this position until 1865. He added wings to the Senate and House of Representatives, as well as the huge central dome of cast iron. He also dabbled in inventions and this ballot box is one of them. The Minutes call it a "beautiful and ingeniously contrived Balloting Box, of Mahogany."[9]

This Victorian round, rotating mahogany box is in the shape of a wheel, fitted continuously around with twelve wedge-shaped cockbeaded drawers with brass ring pulls. Atop the axle is a round covered box 5¾" diameter and 3½" high) which contained the tallies. There is one hole above each drawer for dropping the tallies and each hole has a number (1 through 12) on a round piece of brass on the same level. The wedge-shaped drawers are 5¾" deep and the rotating part is 3½" high. The base is 12¼" in diameter and is 3¼" high. The overall height is 9½" and the overall diameter is 18".[10]

There is a similar balloting box in the State House in Hartford, Connecticut. Each drawer would be marked, perhaps as these are marked, and each act would be assigned a number, as would the candidates for admission to the Society. After the tallies were dropped through the holes, someone would pull the drawers open and count the tallies and announce the results. The tallies would then be stored in the box on top.[11]

1. Archives. I. B. Cohen to L. P. Eisenhart, 21 Feb. 1958; and *Cat. of Insts.*
2. Edward H. Pinto, *Treen and Other Wooden Bygones. An Encyclopaedia and Social History* (London, [1969]), 166.
3. Ibid.
4. Borodin; and *Cat. of Insts.*, 36–37.
5. Archives. B. Dearborn to James Mease; 11 April 1823.
6. Borodin; and *Cat. of Insts.*, 36–37.
7. Min., 4 March 1814.
8. Borodin; and *Cat. of Insts.*, 37. In the *Cat. of Insts.*, this box is wrongly said to have been presented by Thomas U. Walter. The fourth box, as described below, was the one which was presented by Walter.
9. Min., 17 July 1840.
10. Borodin.
11. Archives. Silvio A. Bedini to Murphy D. Smith; 16 May 1986.

Fig. 38b. Ballot Boxes

Spanish-Type Armchair (Fig. 39)

This seventeenth-century type frailero (or religious brothers armchair) dates approximately from 1775–1810 or even from the Spanish colonial revival of 1860–1890. There is no provenance for it whatsoever. It was, however, in Philosophical Hall prior to 1884 for a photograph taken ca. 1883 shows it in the library on the third floor of the Hall. It could have been brought to Philadelphia by the Vaughan family from their estate in the Caribbean area. John Vaughan lived in Philosophical Hall from 1803 until his death in 1841. It might be an un-listed item from his estate which was merely left in the Hall, or an item purchased by the Society. The Society gave $50 on 24 February 1842 to the caretaker of the Hall, William Warren, who inherited some furniture from Vaughan and sold it to the Society.[1]

The chair has a rectangular back of leather which is elaborately embossed

Fig. 39. Spanish-Type Armchair

with heart and tulip devices above an embossed leather seat; all mounted with rosette-headed tacks. The straight arms are raised on square stiles which pass through the seat and are conjoined by a pierced stretcher (chambrana) of chain form. Below is a plain stretcher of square section which is flanked by deeply scalloped lateral stretchers. The height is 41"; the height of the seat is 20"; the width is 26½"; and the arms are 28" high.

Possibly the rosette-headed tacks are replacements, for the chair has had considerable repair: these tacks are not normally found on Spanish fraileros,

nor is the second supporting crossbar in the front. The design on the leather is not Spanish but is more like the design found on South American pieces. Moreover, the "overall dry, simple, rough, provincial nature of the chair" combined with the above, "all point to a South American (probably Ecuador, possibly Peru) origin rather than a Spanish peninsula one."[2]

1. Treas. Recs., 24 Feb. 1842.
2. Borodin; Archives. Richard Ahlborn, Smithsonian Institution, to Murphy D. Smith, 19 May 1986, and, Isadora Rose-de Viejo, Hispanic Society of America, to Murphy D. Smith, 18 Sept. 1986.

BIBLIOGRAPHY

Manuscripts

American Philosophical Society. Archives. Contained in this general subject are:
Archives (a special breakdown), 1768-date.
Edgar P. Richardson, Curator
Minutes, 1766–1928
Treasurer's Records, 1782–1920.

Borodin, David, "Physical Description of Antiques in the American Philosophical Society," 1985.

Converse, Gordon S., "Descriptive Notes on the Clock Made by Edward Duffield at the American Philosophical Society," 1986.

Hanson, Frederick B., and Willman Spawn, "The Hopkinson-APS Chair in the INHP Collection."

Independence National Historical Park. Registrar's descriptions.

"Memorandum—objets donnés ou vendus . . ." Mailliard Family Collection at Yale University Library, Notebook, 1843–1841, relating to the property of Joseph Bonaparte (copy at The Athenaeum of Philadelphia).

Philadelphia Museum of Art. Original Photographs of an Exhibit of Henry Connelly and Ephraim Haines.

Printed Sources

"An Account of the Transit of Mercury over the Sun, on November 9th, 1769, N.S." *Transactions of the American Philosophical Society* (1789), 1:77–83.

––––––. *A Catalogue of Portraits and Other Works of Art in the Possession of the American Philosophical Society. Memoirs of the American Philosophical Society* (1961), 54.

"Armchair from Benjamin Franklin's Library." David Hosack microfilm in the APS Library. Papers, 1797–1826, no. 7.

Barton, William, *Memoirs of the Life of David Rittenhouse . . . Interspersed with Various Notices of Many Distinguished Men* (Philadelphia, 1813).

Bell, Whitfield J., Jr., "I. Minis Hays, Secretary, Librarian, and Benefactor of the American Philosophical Society," *Proceedings of the American Philosophical Society* (1975), 119:401–41.

Burr, Charles W., "Memoir of Dr. Francis X. Dercum." Reprinted from *Medical Life.* (April 1932).

Corner, George Washington, "Henry Allen Moe," *Yearbook, American Philosophical Society*, (1977) 103–109.

Dinsmoor, William B., "Early American Studies in Mediterranean Archeology," *Proceedings of the American Philosophical Society* (1944), 87:90–91.

Hartshorne, Henry, "Memoir of G. B. Wood, M.D., LL.D.," *Proceedings of the American Philosophical Society* (1880–1881), 19:118–52.

Horner, William Macpherson. *Blue Book, Philadelphia Furniture. William Penn to George Washington* (Highland House: [ca. 1977 reprint]).

Ingersoll, Charles J., "Obituary of J. Bonaparte," *Proceedings of the American Philosophical Society* (1854–1858), 6:71–76.

Kelly, Howard A., and Walter L. Burrage, *Dictionary of American Medical Biographies.* (Boston, 1971).

Multhauf, Robert. *A Catalogue of Instruments and Models in the Possession of the American Philosophical Society. Memoirs of the American Philosophical Society* (1961), 53.

Philadelphia Museum of Art. *Philadelphia. Three Centuries of American Art. Bicentennial Exhibition. April 11–October 10, 1976.* Philadelphia Museum of Art [1976].

Pinto, Edward H., *Treen and Other Wooden Bygones. An Encyclopaedia and Social History* (London, [1969]).

Rush, Benjamin, *Eulogium Intended to Perpetuate the Memory of the Late David Rittenhouse, late President of the American Philosophical Society Delivered before the Society in the First Presbyterian Church, in High-Street, Philadelphia, on the 17th December 1796* (Philadelphia, [1796]).

Simpson, George Gaylord, "The Beginnings of Vertebrate Paleontology in North America," *Proceedings of the American Philosophical Society* (1943), 86:130–88.

Swindler, Mary Hamilton, "Another Vase by the Master of the Penthesilea Cylix," *American Journal of Archaeology* (1909), 13:142–50.

Tilghman, William, *An Eulogium in Commemoration of Doctor Caspar Wistar, late President of the American Philosophical Society Held at Philadelphia for Promoting Useful Knowledge, &c.* (Philadelphia, 1818).

Wistar, Caspar, "A Description of the Bones Deposited, by the President, in the Museum of the Society, and Represented in the annexed plates," *Transactions of The American Philosophical Society* (1799), 4:526ff.

The Writings of Thomas Jefferson. Albert Ellery Bergh, ed. (Washington, 1907).

INDEX